HOW CITIES WORK:

AN INTRODUCTION

BY
BARRIE NEEDHAM

Architectural, Planning, and Urban Studies,
University of Aston in Birmingham

PERGAMON PRESS

OXFORD   NEW YORK   TORONTO
SYDNEY   PARIS   FRANKFURT

U.K.	Pergamon Press Ltd., Headington Hill Hall, Oxford OX3 0BW, England
U.S.A.	Pergamon Press Inc., Maxwell House, Fairview Park, Elmsford, New York 10523, U.S.A.
CANADA	Pergamon of Canada Ltd., 75 The East Mall, Toronto, Ontario, Canada
AUSTRALIA	Pergamon Press (Aust.) Pty. Ltd., 19a Boundary Street, Rushcutters Bay, N.S.W. 2011, Australia
FRANCE	Pergamon Press SARL, 24 rue des Ecoles, 75240 Paris, Cedex 05, France
WEST GERMANY	Pergamon Press GmbH, 6242 Kronberg-Taunus, Pferdstrasse 1, Frankfurt-am-Main, West Germany

First edition 1977

Library of Congress Cataloging in Publication Data

Needham, Barrie.
How cities work.

(Urban and regional planning series; v. 17)
Includes bibliographies and index.
1. Cities and towns—Planning—1945. 2. Cities and towns. 3. Cities and towns—Planning—Great Britain. 4. Cities and towns—Great Britain. I. Title. II. Series.
HT166.N42 1977   309.2'62   76-50582
ISBN 0-08-020529-1 (Hard cover)
ISBN 0-08-020528-3 (Flexi cover)

Printed in Great Britain by A. Wheaton & Co., Exeter, Devon

CONTENTS

'We cannot escape any more to the sands or the waves and pretend they are our destiny. We have annihilated time and space, we have furrowed the desert and spanned the sea, only to find at the end of every vista our own unattractive features. What remains for us, whither shall we turn? To the city which we have not yet built, to the unborn polity, to the new heroism.'

> 'We live in a new age in which ... the heroic image is not the nomad wanderer through the desert or over the ocean, but the less exciting figure of the builder who renews the ruined walls of the city. Our temptations are not theirs. ... We are far more likely to become cowards in the face of the tyrant who would compel us to lie in the service of the False City.'

(Forster, E. M., 1965, *Two Cheers for Democracy*, Penguin, p. 273, reviewing Auden, W. H., 1950, *The Enchafed Flood*, Faber, followed by a quotation from p. 125 of that book.)

Two Tales of a City

THIS book tells two stories, one fairly simple and the other more difficult. The simpler story is about how cities work. Most of us live in cities, and we think that we understand the whole city a little and our corner of it a lot—until something unexpected happens in the city that we thought we knew. Then we are confused. The ordinary citizen can enjoy and learn from such surprises or can wallow in outrage at the shocks. The urban planner, however, is supposed to be able to predict how cities will change and, where appropriate, to anticipate the changes. All too often, unfortunately, the workings of cities are a mystery to urban planners. Worse, thinking that they understand the play, planners have many times intervened on the urban stage with unintended results, often turning what would have been a tragedy into a farce.

It is to inform the citizen and to help the planner that I tell this story about how cities work. The more citizens who read this book the better: they might acquire the knowledge which will enable them to challenge the power of those who sit at the centre of the city and who are, alas, often corrupted by that power. The planners whom I would like to help are not only the physical planners who staff town planning departments, but all those who use public powers to try to direct events in the city—transport managers designing bus routes, educational planners proposing new schools, the managers of housing departments, those in the Departments of Employment and of Industry considering training centres or the location of industry, estates surveyors acquiring land for redevelopment, social workers responding to the method of allocating council houses, all those who should be planning together but who find it so difficult to do so.

Many of the best informed citizens of tomorrow will be those who today are studying geography, sociology, urban studies, urban economics. And tomorrow's urban planners are today's students of town planning, transport planning, housing management, social work, public health, estate management, architecture. It is primarily for both those sets of students that I write this book, as an introductory textbook on the city. As such, it is a book of theories rather than a book of facts.

The story of how cities work is one that needs telling, for few other books have attempted so ambitious a task. Alas, I do not tell it perfectly, but you must know that the plot is tangled, the characters many, and their relationships often incestuous.

All who read this book will understand the simple story of how cities work because I have simplified it greatly. The other story is more difficult, but I tell it because it might help other students of the city. It is a methodological story, in which I argue that one method is likely to prove more fruitful than others in understanding cities. Chapter 1 describes the method which I advocate. Chapters 2–10 may then be regarded, methodologically, as tests of whether that method works. Chapter 11 develops the method by applying it to a very difficult subject, public policy-making in cities. Chapter 12 raises a different methodological question by asking: how much can economics help us to understand how cities work? Those who want the simple story only may well miss Chapter 1 (although it is not, I believe, too taxing), and are advised to miss Chapter 12.

The two stories are related. Method (the difficult story) and theory (the simpler story) are not independent: in this case, my choice of method is influenced by the theory, the answer which I give to the question "How do cities work?". As that question is not answered explicitly until Chapter 11, it may be helpful to give a short answer now. Cities work by the interactions of persons, households, firms, public organisations, politicians. Each of these actors has its own motives, which it tries to realise in an environment created by the actions of the other actors: so there is *inter*-action. Often the actors have unequal powers to force the results of their actions on each other. Nevertheless there is not one group of actors which makes the city work or which controls all the workings of the city: the city works, as it were, "on its own". Many undertakings are planned, publicly or privately, but most of the outcomes, each one dependent on the undertakings of a lot of unco-ordinated actors, are unplanned. Sometimes the interactions produce results whereby the city does not work well: parts of it are abandoned, its arteries clog, death rates are high. So, often the city works badly. But most cities do work, continue to function, largely as the result of human ingenuity and adaptiveness to continually changing circumstances.

That is my answer to the question, "How do cities work?". (There are other answers, mentioned briefly in Chapter 11.) And that answer influences the method which I recommend for studying cities, the method of studying partial urban systems, sets of interactions.

There is one important aspect of the working of cities, one chapter of the first story, which I have not described. That is the way in which land and buildings are developed—how and why the use of land changes, buildings are built, buildings are put to changed uses. So in this book we talk generally about the demand for land and buildings and the supply of land and buildings, but the details of how that demand and supply result in buildings being constructed and used we do not discuss: Chapters 5, 6 and 7 approach nearest to that subject but do not reach it. The reason for the omission is not that the method, the second story, is inapplicable to it: on the contrary, the method fits it well. Rather it is that the subject is big enough to require a separate book.

One final word of introduction. I use the words *towns* and *cities* indiscriminately to refer to what would be more accurately called *urban settlements*. That word, however, is too long and ugly for use throughout a book.

At the end of most chapters is a list of some books for further reading. That list is not exhaustive: it would be an impossible and useless task to make it so. The purpose of the lists is to enable readers easily to study further the main ideas in the chapters: for that reason I have tried to recommend books which are not much more difficult than this one, I have not referred to articles in periodicals, I have been specific about which parts of the books to read,

I have kept the lists short, and there are a few books each of which is recommended for several of the chapters.

My colleagues in the department have always been ready to help me with ideas and suggestions, in particular Paul Truelove and Peter Hills. Also I have benefited greatly from discussing Chapter 11 with Chris Paris at the Centre for Urban and Regional Studies, Birmingham University: the fact that he disagrees with much of it in no way belittles the help he has given me. I want to thank Mrs. Elaine Kirby for typing the manuscript and the Communications Media Unit of Aston University for drawing some of the diagrams. I gratefully acknowledge permission to reproduce diagrams as follows:

Fig. 3.3	The University of Wales Press.
Fig. 7.3	Liverpool University Press.
Figs. 8.2 and 8.3	Her Majesty's Stationery Office.
Fig. 8.4	City of Liverpool.
Figs. 9.1, 9.2, 9.3, 9.4, 9.5	City of Birmingham
Fig. 9.6	Architecture and Planning Publications Ltd.
Fig. 10.1	John Wiley and Sons Ltd.

CHAPTER 1

Studying the City

We shall study the city as a set of interactions between individuals, and take as our text:

> "A city is a complex living system. Its anatomy and composition can be studied and analysed like any other living system. Certain parts can be distinguished from the mass and identified so that eventually each microscopic element of the system can be assigned to a part. The interactions between these parts may then be traced over time. ... However, a living system may be subdivided by many different methods, and independent observers find it difficult to agree as to which will ultimately yield the most information of a useful sort. This study of cities starts with those pieces or elements which yield the least amount of ambiguity and disagreement at the start—the names and addresses of individual humans and organisations. It considers the transactions between these unitary elements, and especially the messages which make up an important share of the interaction within a complete transaction." (Meier, 1962, p. 1).

A SYSTEMS APPROACH

A system is, as all the textbooks agree, a set of connected parts or things. But there is not agreement on the meaning of a "systems approach" so we must start by describing some of the ways in which the term is used.

One systems approach is: study the whole set (i.e. the system), not its parts, because this approach is methodologically more fruitful.

Another systems approach is: study the whole set, not its component parts, because the whole is greater than the sum of its parts. So it is logically wrong (not just methodologically unhelpful) to study the parts. (This approach could be called "holism"—see later—or the Gestalt approach.)

Yet another systems approach is: if we study the whole rather than the parts, we find that some of the properties of the whole system are similar whether we are studying a city, a biological organism, a firm, or any other system. Those similarities are the subject of general systems theory. So if we study the whole we can apply to it knowledge from general systems theory. (On the above three approaches see Emery, 1969.)

A different systems approach is: we shall look at the parts, not the whole. But it is still a systems approach because we shall not forget the connections between the parts. This approach may be called "systems analysis" (see Catanese and Steiss, 1971, chap. 1).

For reasons which will be argued later, I do not recommend a systems approach which looks at the whole (the set, or the system) , rather than at the parts. Instead I recommend a systems approach which looks at the parts, but which does not forget the connections between the parts. So my approach is based on E. M. Forster's text "Only connect". His sermon (quoted here out of context) continues, "Live in fragments no longer". The aim of this book is to teach about *interactions* and *inter-relationships* between urban components and activities. And the approach is modelled on Popper's statement that the main task of the social sciences is "analysing the unintended social repercussions of intentional human actions" (Popper, 1966, p. 96). What are the consequences of the actions of the individual actors in the urban drama, when those actions combine in unintended ways?

AN ECOLOGICAL APPROACH

To what are we going to take a systems approach?—to an understanding of why the city is as it is, why it changes, how to change it, and some of the effects of changing it. And, besides the systems approach to searching for this understanding, we shall take another complementary, approach, viz. an ecological approach.

Ecology is briefly defined as the study of the interactions between an organism and its environment. Applied to the search for an understanding of the city built and used by man, the ecological approach looks at the interactions between the *activities* of men and the *spaces* in which the activities take place (see Sprout and Sprout, 1965).

In a little more detail, men's activities take place in spaces. They may be naturally provided spaces (e.g. men bathing in the sea) but more often they are *adapted spaces* (e.g. buildings). In the latter case, man has adapted the natural environment to his own use: so men's activities act on the physical environment. But the reverse may happen also: the spaces act on the activities (as when you adapt your activities to a given building). So there is *interaction* between activities and spaces.

Men want to *communicate* also, either by passing messages between each other, or by sending goods, or by travelling themselves. The communications take place along *channels*, which may be naturally provided (e.g. rivers), but which more often are adapted (e.g. roads, telephones). Again, there is interaction between communications and channels.

But the interactions do not stop there. For example, channels may affect communications which may affect activities which may affect spaces, as when a new motorway causes a firm to re-route its lorries, then to consider establishing a separate distribution depot near a motorway junction, then to have a warehouse built there. (This ecological approach is described more fully in McLoughlin, 1969, chap. 1.) Such an ecological way of looking at the connections and interactions between activities, communications, spaces, and channels is obviously consistent with and complementary to the type of systems approach which we shall be taking in this book.

THE APPROACH OF INDIVIDUALISM

Popper (1966) distinguishes between "methodological individualism" and "methodological collectivism". The individualist approach analyses social relations, institutions, and traditions in terms of the interactions between individuals acting in certain social situations. The collectivist approach analyses in terms of social classes, or organisations, or societies, acting as wholes or entities (as, for example, analysing industrial relations in terms of two social classes in conflict, rather than in terms of individuals behaving in certain social situations).

In this book we take the individualist approach, for two reasons. The first is that individuals are more easily observed than groups, indeed that groups or collectivities can be observed only through individuals. The second is that, in my opinion, people are more important than groups, and that to analyse at the level of groups is to court the danger of forgetting about, or being insensitive to, individuals. (For a fuller comparison of these two approaches see Needham and Faludi, 1973.) So it is that the interactions which we study in this book are interactions between individuals. (Two disclaimers! One is that methodological individualism does not say that sociology can be reduced to psychology. The other is that the individualist approach does not rule out talking about collectivities—such as the labour force, or employers, or motorists—as long as we do not give to those collectivities identities or wills which can properly belong only to their members.)

The combination of those three approaches is nicely exemplified in a story told by McLoughlin (1962, pp. 29–34). It is an everyday story told in everyday language of everyday city folk, starting with Mr. A the proprietor of With-it Weatherware Ltd. His firm operates on the edge of the city centre, until changing circumstances persuade Mr. A to move a little further out, into an inner-ring suburb. That is the last straw for Mrs. B who has lived in that suburb all her life and has seen it go downhill. So she, with her married son, moves into a bungalow in a nicer residential area. In so doing, they add to the already growing population of that area, and when Mrs. B junior applies to join the local tennis club, that is just another example of the overloading of facilities in the burgeoning suburb. What is to be done? Listen next week! Better still, make up the next episode yourself: you will find it easy if you take a systems approach, an ecological approach, and an individualist approach.

URBAN SYSTEMS

If we understood the whole urban system completely (something which, I shall argue later, is logically impossible) we could represent it diagrammatically (see Fig. 1.1(a)). If we want to study the *whole* system we must draw a boundary to include all the important con-nections (see Fig. 1.1(b)). If we want to study a part only of the

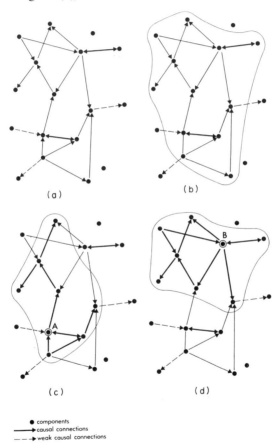

Fig. 1. (a) Diagrammatic representation of a system. (b) The boundary of the whole system. (c) The boundary of a partial system. (d) The boundary of another partial system.

system (Component A), not forgetting its connections with other parts of the system, we need to look only at those connections and other parts which are relevant. That defines our partial system for us (see Fig. 1.1(c)). If we want to study another part (B), the system which we need to study is different (see Fig. 1.1(d)).

The systems approach which we are taking in this book is to study only those parts and those connections between parts which are necessary for understanding the problem at hand. That means that we shall not try to study the whole urban system, but partial urban systems. It means also that the system is defined by reference to the problem. If the problem is stated in terms of a particular part or a particular connection, then all those other parts and connections which are related to the problem part or connection must be included in the system.

That means that the definition of the system is *ad hoc*—i.e. it varies according to the problem (a point clearly recognised in systems analysis). But although the definition of the system is *ad hoc* in that it depends on which part or connection you start from, the choice of other parts to include is not arbitrary. For the other parts which must be included are all those which affect or are affected by the problem part. But how do we know about those connections? By theory, which gives *causal* explanations (and hence which tells us what affects what: see Ryan, 1970, chap. 4). So the problem determines the starting point for defining the system, and theory determines what should be included in the system, given the starting point.

An example from theory will illustrate that. Suppose the problem is: why do racial minorities often live concentrated together in inner city areas? One starting point would be: racial minorities. Then theory suggests that we include in our system: discrimination by racial majorities, cultural identities and differences, occupational skills, etc.

Another starting point could be: residential location. Then theory suggests that we should include in our system: locational differences in housing costs, income available for housing, building society practices, location of workplaces, transport routes and costs, etc.

(Note how this type of systems approach often cuts right across so-called "disciplinary boundaries". That is, by trying to include all the relevant relationships you cannot stay inside the discipline of economics, or sociology, or geography, etc. In my opinion, that should not be resisted.)

Let us take another example, this time from policy. Suppose the problem is: how to reduce the level of unemployment. The starting point is the rate of unemployment. Theory suggests that we look at: demand for labour, demand for goods and services, level of aggregate expenditure, size of budget deficit, government fiscal policy. This example is taken from Lipsey (1966, p. 837), where he applies a systems-analysis approach as follows:

$$\text{government policy} \rightarrow \text{an instrumental variable} \rightarrow \text{any number of intermediate variables} \rightarrow \text{the policy variable}$$

The policy variable is that in terms of which the problem is stated: unemployment is too high, so the policy variable is the rate of unemployment. That is our starting point for defining the relevant system. We work outwards from it, specifying chains of causal connections, until we come to a variable which can be influenced by public powers: in this case, the size of the budget deficit. So the instrumental variable is that which can be influenced directly by the government policy, and which will then influence indirectly the policy variable. In such a way is a system defined around a problem. The connections between the variables (or parts of the system) are provided by economic theory. If the theory is wrong, the policy will not work. If the theory is right the policy should work.

But what about the side effects? Lipsey's diagram does not show them, but they must be considered in any policy making. "The natural tendency", says Wilson (1974, p. 7) "is to try to solve...problems, but usually in an oversimplistic way, without any detailed understanding of the problems and their *interdependence*, and without any ability to predict the consequences of implementing the solutions." Wilson's attempt to understand interdependencies is the same as ours to understand all the interactions within the relevant system.

Other examples of urban systems are the *activity systems* upon which Chapin concentrates (Chapin, 1965). He defines them as "behaviour patterns of individuals, families, institutions, and firms, which occur in spatial patterns that have meaning in planning for land use" (p. 224). (The danger with Chapin's approach is the implication that to define systems by starting with activities always produces the most useful systems for land-use planning. For some land-use planning problems, it might be more helpful to take a different starting point.)

Other examples of urban systems are, of course, to be found in the following chapters of this book. So it may be helpful to describe the basis on which these partial, *ad hoc*, systems were chosen, and other systems excluded. Briefly, those urban systems were chosen which are (in my opinion) most important for urban planning. So the systems include those interactions which the planner can use (e.g. how can we influence the number of people living in an area? by controlling the number of jobs in the area), and those interactions, ignorance of which can be most harmful to the planned (e.g. if we ignore the interaction between housing areas, we may improve one housing area only to worsen another).

The advantages of taking this type of systems approach should by now be becoming apparent. In the search for better theory, we are looking for correct causal explanations. These are cause-and-effect relationships, sometimes long and complicated causal chains. An explicit systems approach means that we seek out the cause-and-effect relationships, wherever the search takes us (and even across disciplinary boundaries). In the search for better policy, we are trying to find how to use powers to resolve problems. What powers will affect the problems, and in what ways? Will there be any unintended consequences of using the powers in that way? And if the problem is alleviated, will the improvement have any unexpected effects? An explicit systems approach helps us to answer those questions. (And in Chapter 2 are given examples of where planning went wrong because it ignored important interactions.)

But there is one snare along the systems path which must be pointed out. It is that to talk about "changes in urban systems" is ambiguous. It could mean that the structure of the system (i.e. the relationships between its parts) changes. Or it could mean that the structure is unchanged, that one part changes, and that as a result (because it is a system) other parts change. An example of the second type of change is where an increase in the number of people with a given skill causes the wage rate earned by people with that skill to change, which causes some of those people to look for jobs elsewhere. An example of the first type of change is what would happen in that labour market if there was a huge and rapid technological change.

Much confusion can be caused by not distinguishing between those two types of change (e.g. what is meant by a "dynamic urban system"? See Popper, 1964, section 27). In particular, the consequences of the first type of change are unpredictable, whereas the second type of change has predictable consequences. This book will talk about changes in urban systems mainly in the second sense.

DIFFICULTIES WITH STUDYING PARTIAL SYSTEMS

In Chapters 5, 6, and 7 the limitations of our chosen approach become very obvious. We have chosen to study *partial* systems and not to try to understand the whole urban system: as a result we study in Chapter 5 the interactions between people and housing, in Chapter 6 the interactions between people and industry, and in Chapter 7 the interactions between people and commercial services. Yet it is obvious that if (for example) people and houses interact, and if people and jobs interact, then houses and jobs interact. And casual observation confirms that: if a firm expands, it attracts more people to the town, who require more housing.

We have chosen to study partial systems, and here already we find interactions between partial systems. What are we to do? We must not allow ourselves to hunt the chimera of a theory of the complete urban system: that we foreswore earlier. The answer is to define new systems which incorporate the problem we are trying to solve. For example, if the housing demand created by new employment is our problem, then we need to study the system of people/jobs/houses. That system is larger than either the people/jobs, or the people/houses system, and hence is more difficult to understand: but it is nowhere near being the complete urban system.

Yet even such attempts to widen the urban system we study take us beyond current knowledge. And in practice, urban and regional planners want to know about even bigger urban systems—about, for example, the interactions between people, houses, jobs, and services. It is instructive to see how practising planners have managed to work with inadequate theory, for it shows that the limitations of studying partial systems need not cripple practice.

Some planners start with *industry*. So the Lowry model (Lowry, 1964) starts with a given increase in basic industry. From that are predicted population and commercial services. And the South Hampshire model (Rhodes, 1970) started by assuming unconstrained industrial growth in the sub-region, from that predicting population, housing, and land uses.

Many planners start with *population*. For example, the aim might be to try to stop the net emigration of people from the town. What industry is necessary for that? The plan for the expansion of Ipswich (Shankland, Cox and Associates, 1968) started with the proposal to bring 70,000 people into Ipswich by 1981. How many jobs will be needed? And what commercial services, recreational facilities, and housing will that population require? (Most new town plans are produced in that way.)

Some planners try to look at both industry and population together. So they might ask the following series of questions. What is the likely natural increase of the present population? What is the likely migration if present trends continue? What is the likely growth of jobs if present trends continue? Are labour supply and labour demand thus calculated the same? If not, is the difference within the margins of error of any forecast? If not, is there too much labour? If so, do we want to attract more industry, or do we want to revise the migration forecasts? Or is there too little labour? If so, do we want to attract more immigrants, or accept that industry will grow more slowly than forecast? (see, for example, West Midlands Regional Study, 1971).

What planners would like to be able to do is to use a well-tried theory of the relevant urban system (e.g. the system of people/jobs/houses) in order to make conditional predictions of the state of the system, given different assumptions and different inputs. But such theories of larger urban systems are not yet available, so planners have to use devices such as those described above. In this book we want to describe the smaller urban systems, knowledge of which is necessary for such devices to be used.

DIFFICULTIES WITH STUDYING SYSTEMS AS WHOLES

Earlier I recommended a systems approach for this subject which looked at parts and their interconnections, rather than one which started with whole systems. It may be helpful to discuss some of the theoretical reasons for this.

One reason is the logical impossibility of defining a whole system. "If we wish to study a thing, we are bound to select certain aspects of it. It is not possible for us to observe or to describe a whole piece of the world, or a whole piece of nature; in fact, not even the smallest whole piece may be so described, since all description is necessarily selective." (Popper, 1964, section 23: see also Bailey, 1975, chap. 1.) In practice, we select by defining systems around some starting point, e.g. the system for providing and allocating housing, the system for moving goods and people. That is the systems approach which we have decided to adopt. .

If we are looking for *functional theories*, then we have to try to look at systems as wholes. Functional explanations of cities explain urban processes in terms of the necessity of maintaining certain goals of the urban system. See, for example, Harvey's interpretation of urbanism using Marxist methodology, in which he describes Marxist holism as, "The totality seeks to shape the parts so that each part functions to preserve the existence and general structure of the whole" (Harvey, 1973, p. 289). Such functional explanations are teleological: an event is explained by the necessity of achieving the effect which it causes. (For a discussion of the difficulties with teleological theories see Ryan, 1970, chap. 8.) Such explanations are valid for systems which have been designed to achieve a system goal (e.g. a firm) and for systems where there is a mechanism in control of the parts (e.g. the human physical body). But a city is not such a system. There are not city-wide goals which constrain people to act in particular ways: the state of the city is the unintended result of many individuals pursuing their own goals. So functional theories of cities are not acceptable (which does not exclude functional *analogies* of cities, such as Schnore (1971) comparing a city to an organism). So the search for functional theories is not a valid reason for trying to study the urban system as a whole.

Beware, therefore, of general or comprehensive theories of cities! For example, Parry Lewis (1971) claims to be moving towards a "comprehensive" model of the urban system, but that turns out to be a model that includes the interactions between a town's *major* activities and characteristics, not *all* of the town's activities and characteristics (although it does try to include more activities than are included in most partial urban systems). And what are the major activities for one problem (e.g. traffic and land use problems) may not be important for another problem (e.g. unemployment problems). So Parry Lewis's comprehensive model is really a big partial model of the urban system. And that is true of all comprehensive or general theories (unless we use Batty's perverse definitions of partial models which simulate one land use or activity and general models which simulate two or more—Batty, 1972).

"Planners are now prisoners of the discovery that in the city everything affects everything else" says Lowry (1965). It is true that in the city everything affects everything else, because if it is, then surely we need to study the complete urban system? It probably is true, but the conclusion does not follow. To say "everything affects everything else" is as true, and as trivial, as to say that my weight changes when an aircraft passes overhead. What we need to know are what effects are *significant* and what *are not*. Without such knowledge we cannot simplify, and we are in effect prisoners, trapped in the impossibility of studying the town as a whole. With such knowledge we can simplify, and develop partial theories which work. It is ironical that ignorance often leads us to attempt the most difficult tasks first and that more knowledge is needed before the folly of doing that can be seen (see, for example, *Requiem for large-scale models* by Lee, 1973).

INDEX TO REFERENCES IN CHAPTER 1

BAILEY, J., 1965, *Social Theory for Planning*, Routledge & Kegan Paul, London.

BATTY, M., 1972, "Recent developments in land-use modelling", *Urban Studies*, vol. 9, no. 2.

CATANESE, A. J. and STEISS, A. W., 1970, *Systemic Planning: Theory and Explanation*, Heath Lexington Books, Lexington.

CHAPIN, F. S., 1965, *Urban Land-use Planning*, University of Illinois, 2nd ed.

EMERY, F. E., 1969 (ed.), *Systems Thinking*, Penguin, Harmondsworth.

HARVEY, D., 1973, *Social Justice and the City*, Arnold, London.

LEE, D. B., 1973, "Requiem for large-scale models", *Journal of the American Institute of Planners*, vol. 39, no. 3.

LIPSEY, R. G., 1966, *Introduction to Positive Economics*, Weidenfeld & Nicholson, London, 2nd ed.

LOWRY, I. S., 1964, *Model of Metropolis*, Rand Corporation, Santa Monica.

LOWRY, I. S., 1965, "A short course in model design", *Journal of the American Institute of Planners*, vol. 31, no. 2.

McLOUGHLIN, J. B., 1969, *Urban and Regional Planning: a Systems Approach*, Faber & Faber, London.

MEIER, R. L., 1962, *A Communications Theory of Urban Growth*, M.I.T. Press.

NEEDHAM, B. and FALUDI, A., 1973, "Planning and the public interest", *Journal of the Royal Town Planning Institute*, vol. 59, no. 4.

PARRY LEWIS, J., 1971, "Towards a comprehensive urban simulation model", Papers of the 1971 Urban Economics Conference, Centre for Environmental Studies, London.

POPPER, K. R., 1964, *The Poverty of Historicism*, Harper & Row, New York.

POPPER, K. R., 1966, *The Open Society and its Enemies*, Routledge & Kegan Paul, London.

RHODES, T., 1970, "The quantitative framework of the structure plan", *Journal of the Town Planning Institute*, vol. 56, no. 6.

RYAN, A., 1970, *Philosophy of the Social Sciences*, Macmillan, London.

SCHNORE, L. F., 1971, "The city as a social organism", in Bourne, L. S. (ed.) *Internal Structure of the City*, OUP, New York.

SHANKLAND, COX & ASSOCIATES, 1968, *Ipswich Draft Basic Plan*, HMSO, London.

SPROUT, H. and SPROUT, M., 1965, *The ecological perspective on Human Affairs*, Princeton University Press.

WEST MIDLANDS REGIONAL STUDY, 1971, *A Developing Strategy for the West Midlands*, Birmingham.

WILSON, A. G., 1974, *Urban and Regional Models in Geography and Planning*, John Wiley, London.

FURTHER READING FOR CHAPTER 1

BEISHON, J. and PETERS, G. (eds.), 1972, *Systems Behaviour*, Harper & Row, London, sections I and V.

HALL, P., 1974, *Urban and Regional Planning*, Penguin, Harmondsworth, chapter 10.

Human Activity Systems, 1974, The Open University Press, Bletchley (T242 3).

McLoughlin, J. B., 1969, *Urban and Regional Planning: a Systems Approach*, Faber & Faber, London, chapters 1–4.

Popper, K. R., 1964, *The Poverty of Historicism*, Harper & Row, New York.

Ryan, A., 1970, *Philosophy of the Social Sciences*, Macmillan, London.

Sprout, H. and Sprout, M., 1965, *The Ecological Perspective on Human Affairs*, Princeton University Press.

CHAPTER 2

Examples of Planning Mistakes

INTRODUCTION

In the previous chapter we said that a systems approach can help the planner to avoid mistakes, by making it easier to take account of the interactions between urban components. In this chapter, that claim is supported by examples of planning mistakes, where the cause of the mistakes was ignorance of important interactions. The interactions were ignored, either because no one knew about them at the time (as, for example, doctors did not know in earlier times that sewage in drinking water could cause cholera) or because the planners did not use the available knowledge. It is not fair to blame practitioners for inadequate theory, it is fair to blame them for not using adequate theory. For whatever reasons important interactions were ignored, the results were that the consequences of the planners' actions were not correctly predicted or that the full extent and significance of the predicted consequences were not appreciated.

(There is no implication in this chapter that ignorance about interactions is the only or the most serious cause of planning mistakes. Such mistakes will also be caused by planners using incorrect facts, trying to achieve the wrong things, failing to forecast the future (as distinct from failing to predict the consequences of known changes), and so on.)

PLANNING BLIGHT

Planning blight is an unintended result of the interaction between the actions of planners and the area which is being planned.

15

After planners have chosen an area for action (e.g. for road works, redevelopment, improvement) it is often many years before the planning implementation starts, whether it be building works, one-way schemes, declaration of conservation areas, or anything else. During this delay, the planners make (and avoid making) many decisions. These decisions have unintended effects on the area, usually causing it to deteriorate physically: the effects are then called "planning blight". Sometimes planning blight helps the planning authority, by causing the value of the properties to fall, thus making acquisition cheaper. (Then one is tempted to be cynical and to wonder whether planning blight really is unintentional.) Other times, planning blight hinders the planning authority by making the plan objectives more difficult to achieve.

Davies's study of planning in Newcastle-upon-Tyne (Davies, 1972) describes planning blight which hindered the local authority (besides putting many people to unnecessary expense, movement, and distress). The place was Rye Hill, an inner city area of nineteenth century terraces. The plan was to improve the houses and the local environment, a "comprehensive revitalisation", by acquiring houses compulsorily if necessary. (Another case study of planning blight can be found in Dennis, 1972.)

It was the way the Council worked that caused planning blight. One important cause was the Council policy of buying houses by agreement whenever a willing owner stepped forward. The richer owner-occupiers, who could use the money from the sale to buy elsewhere, sold early to the Council. The poorer owner-occupiers did not want to sell because the value of their houses was too low to enable them to buy elsewhere. The landlords did not want to sell because they were making a lot of money from their properties. As a result, the number of owner-occupiers fell (from 51% in 1962 to 15% in 1967 in one area of 200 houses), leaving behind as owners poorer owner-occupiers, private landlords, and the local authority. These owners did not maintain the houses as well as the richer owner-occupiers had done. Another cause of planning blight was the Council policy of not modernising the houses as it purchased them, but keeping them "in cold storage" awaiting a "phased comprehensive programme of implementation" (the Council's term). Such houses in cold storage were quickly attacked by vandals.

The effects of the ensuing planning blight on the residents of Rye Hill were extra expense and great distress. On the plan, the blight had the following effects. Modernisation costs increased because the properties had not been maintained during the delay. Many of the owner-occupiers could not afford their share of the costs because the costs had increased and because the richer owner-occupiers had moved away. Many of the houses originally proposed for improvement decayed so much that they had to be demolished and replaced. The character of the area, which, it had been hoped, would be retained by revitalisation, drained away.

Davies concludes " ... plans must be based on a sensitive knowledge of the movements of the 'invisible hand' (i.e. how the market works) and must be based on *that* knowledge and not deduced from some irrelevant set of half-examined notions ... " (p. 217).

THE DEATH AND LIFE OF GREAT AMERICAN CITIES

In the introduction to her now-famous attack on American city planning, Jacobs writes (1965, p. 13), "I shall be writing about how cities work in real life ... " and she argues that much of the city planning in the United States of the 1950's ignored how cities really work.

For example, planners build streets for cars, try to keep people off the streets, plan houses which turn their backs on the pavements, try to get children off the streets into parks. That ignores, says Jacobs, the fact that streets and pavements perform a vital function: they keep the city safe. "The point of ... the social life of city side-walks is precisely that they are public" (p. 66). (It is this argument which Newman (1972) developed later in his book *Defensible Space.*) The result of the planners' success in getting people off the streets is that the *trust* on which a city is built, and which pavements help to sustain, evaporates.

As another example, Jacobs argues that the essence of cities is social and economic *diversity*, that diversity requires certain physical conditions, and that it is just those conditions which city planners are so keen to eradicate. The result of such planning is that cities become poorer, socially and economically. The argument for diversity is an argument for variety and innovation in industry, commerce, consumption, culture, and entertainment. Such can only be provided by many small enterprises, and small enterprises can only afford to operate in cities. "Cities are the natural homes of supermarkets and standard movie houses *plus* delicatessens, viennese bakeries, foreign groceries, art movies, and so on..." (p. 158). But as well as the size of a city, small enterprises require four *physical conditions* within the city: each district must serve many functions, city blocks must be small, each district must contain buildings varying in age and condition, the concentration of people must be sufficiently dense. Yet what do city planners do, not only in the United States but also in Britain? They segregate land uses, rationalise street patterns, propose large-scale redevelopments, reduce housing densities. The results are familiar: the small trader retires, back-yard industries are forbidden, small industrial and commercial premises disappear (see, for example, Cameron and Johnson, 1969, for the Scottish experience). Where, in a redeveloped city centre can you buy second-hand books, fishing tackle, sheet music, nuts and bolts, tripe? Jacobs warns us to remember to count the cost to the city of this loss of diversity.

SOME ECONOMIC CONSEQUENCES OF REGIONAL PLANNING IN LONDON

Planners usually take a physical approach to problems in London and to their solution. The problems are physical—overcrowding at the centre, congestion of the arteries, internal decay, environmental decline, dreary suburbs, long work journeys, poor housing, and so on. To this set of physical problems there is an orthodox set of physical planning solutions. The metropolitan settlement pattern should be restructured, with fewer living in the old core of London and more living in separate settlements outside the conurbation, settlements with associated jobs so that residents do not have to travel into London for work. There should be a network of radial, tangential, and orbital roads with improved radial railway lines and an integrated public transport system in the conurbation. There should be a large-scale programme of urban renewal, together with sympathetic conservation policies (see, for example, the Greater London Development Plan, 1969).

Eversley (1972) criticises that physical planning approach, not because the diagnosis is wrong, nor because the solutions are bad, but because the solutions contribute to two further economic problems which are ignored. These exascerbated problems are the rising costs of construction and of public services in the city, and a static income from which to pay those rising costs. Eversley argues that the mistake lies in not having predicted these economic consequences of physical planning, and that measures should be taken (such as changing the rating system), not to change the physical proposals, but to alleviate the economic damage they are causing.

Costs are rising in London for several reasons. As cities grow older their structures become more complex above and below ground, so construction becomes more difficult. Buildings are growing obsolete more quickly. Productivity in public services is rising more slowly than in manufacturing or in some private services. All these things are causing the costs of construction and of public services to rise. The current regional planning for London is fuelling this fire in the following ways. Some of the public provision which has to be made in a city is not proportional to the resident population of the city (e.g. public transport, fire services, police services): so, as the population falls, expenditure on such services cannot fall as fast, and costs per resident increase. As population densities fall, transport costs per person increase because to contact others you have to travel further. As the population declines, some public transport facilities which were provided many years ago for a bigger population are used below their maximum capacity. And as people and jobs decentralise, public transport becomes less efficient and journeys grow longer.

Many of the extra costs fall, directly or indirectly, on the local authority (the Greater London Council or the London boroughs).

Yet the ability of the G.L.C. to pay extra costs is weak: its rateable base is growing more slowly than are rateable bases in the rest of the country. That weak financial base also can be partly attributed to the regional planning for London. For example, the movement of people and jobs out of the city reduces the number of hereditaments remaining (i.e. properties on which rates are levied): also, the decentralisation reduces the competition for properties, hence their values, hence London's rateable base. The rateable values of properties depend also on personal incomes, a direct dependence for housing, an indirect dependence for buildings in which goods and services are produced for local consumption. And personal incomes in the G.L.C. area are declining relative to personal incomes in the rest of the South East, partly because the regional planning policies for London encourage richer people to leave that city.

Those, says Eversley, are unforeseen consequences of the regional planning now being applied to London. And the consequences could be serious: "One of the major changes in urban social geography (in London) is the emergence of large areas of continuous poverty or at least relative deprivation.... If this kind of area grows and coalesces with others, the friction it generates may further accelerate the outward movement of the upwardly mobile."

HOUSING AND INDUSTRY IN INNER CITY AREAS

In Chapter 5 we shall explain that the supply of labour by people and the demand for labour by industry must be in rough balance, and that the balance must be not only in the total amount of labour but also in the type of labour. For example, a supply of 1000 workers is not going to balance a demand for 1000 workers if the supply is of people with clerical skills and the demand is for skilled workers to make machine tools. There is evidence from local authority redevelopment in some parts of inner London that this detailed balance has been ignored, that the consequences of the housing and the industrial policies have not been predicted in enough detail, and that the interaction between those two policies has not been studied. (The evidence comes from work in Lambeth—IAS/LA/4, 1975 and IAS/

LA/6, 1975—and from student projects carried out from the Polytechnic, Regent Street, 1968/9.)

The ring of development around the commercial core of London has contained many manufacturing plants, often employing skilled workers. The factories were in old buildings on cramped sites where rents were low. Plans for such areas usually designate broad zones for housing and a few small sites for industry: moreover, the old factories were usually surrounded by housing and so could be classified as "non-conforming uses" and bought out before any redevelopment started. If the existing firms had wanted to stay in such areas they would have had to move onto the land newly designated for industry and to rebuild there at high costs. Moreover, the new factories would have been at lower densities than the old factories, so even if the same amount of industrial land had been designated as had existed previously, that new land would have been able to accommodate fewer workers. The result of such planning on industry is to speed up the process which is occurring for other reasons, the process whereby existing firms close down or move to the outskirts of London and neighbouring small towns. For example, it was estimated in 1974 that Lambeth Borough's redevelopment programme would displace 93,000 square metres of industrial floorspace and 3000 jobs (IAS/LA/7, 1975).

The town planning departments which are responsible are not ignorant of those consequences, and their answer is: Don't worry! Employment in central London will provide the necessary jobs. We know that the number of jobs in central London is falling, but it is falling more slowly than the number of workers living around the centre of London.

As well as affecting industry, town planning in the inner areas has affected housing. Such areas traditionally contained working-class housing, privately owned or privately rented, accommodating people at a high density. Redevelopment is replacing that with local authority rented housing, usually at a lower density. Moreover, the housing policy of the older London boroughs is usually to give priority to those families who have lived in the area a long time, those who are known to be respectable and reliable, those with families, and those who have owned houses which the local authority has cleared.

Those policies for industry and for housing are inconsistent, and the inconsistency can be described by relating people's occupations and incomes to the types of housing which are available and obtainable. Housing policies for the inner areas of London are resulting in a growing proportion of the housing being owned by the local authority and rented mainly to manual workers with traditional skills. Industrial policy has placed reliance on jobs supplied by central London: but what types of jobs are these? They are jobs for highly-trained professional workers (e.g. accountants), for less-skilled non-manual workers (e.g. secretaries, sales staff), and to a smaller extent jobs for less-skilled or unskilled manual workers in the service sector (e.g. cleaners, porters, catering and hotel workers). Those jobs are usually filled by people who want to and can afford to buy their own homes, or who need to or want to rent but cannot get council housing so rent privately. For example, professional workers normally own their own homes. Clerical workers might aspire to do that, but usually cannot afford to buy in inner London: if they are the young women in such great demand for secretarial jobs in central London they will not qualify for council housing so will have to rent privately.

As a result, housing is provided for families whose men supply labour for which there is little demand as a result of the industrial policy. And industry demands labour from people for whom housing is not available as a result of the housing policy.

The results of that inconsistency are unintended and undesirable. Non-manual and skilled manual workers, who can afford to move, are leaving inner London. Other manual workers who might like to move out to places where there are more jobs are unable to do so, because the housing in outer London is unobtainable by them: as a result, such manual workers remain in inner London where many of them suffer unemployment, unstable employment, or low earnings. The richer owner occupiers and the private tenants are fighting in parts of inner London for what remains of the private housing there, with the victory going to the richest: the fruits of victory can be seen in the "gentrification" of areas like Barnsbury and Camberwell, where rich people are buying houses which previously provided cheap rented accommodation for poor people. The private tenants, unable to find enough housing, cannot supply the labour which the local authorities and others so desperately need. And the characteristics, and some of the problems, of inner London spread outwards.

THE LIMITATIONS OF PHYSICAL PLANNING

Much of the planning that takes place in our towns and cities tries to have its effect by changing the physical environment. Town and country planning controls the uses of land and buildings, much transport planning is by providing or controlling roads, much housing planning is by building, improving, or allocating dwellings. So planners are trying to tackle some public problems by changing land, buildings, spaces, and channels.

Such planning is based upon a theory, explicit or implicit, about the relationship between public problems and the physical environment. (The ecological approach discussed in Chapter 1 is obviously relevant to this.) If that theory is wrong, the planners will make mistakes.

One of the theories about the physical environment and human behaviour and activities is called physical determinism. In its strong form, this is the theory that behaviour is determined by the physical environment; in a weaker form, it says that behaviour can be changed and manipulated by changing the physical environment.

The theory of physical determinism, if true, has obvious relevance to physical planning: provide the right physical environment, and everything will be alright, there will be no more public problems. And the theory has been so used. For example, Crosby (1965, p. 83) writes: "It is only by an achievement on the scale of Regent's Park that an environment of sufficient power is created to change the community's way of life. There is no doubt that these places (Crosby mentions Edinburgh New Town, Bath, and Bloomsbury) exerted a profoundly civilising effect on their inhabitants, and they still do so—sophisticated sins, but no vulgar brawling."

In practice, Kuper (1953) studied how architects used the theory, by designing local authority housing estates in order to create neigh-

bourly contacts and attitudes. And we can see, by studying development plans, that town planners have tried to solve problems of too
few jobs by zoning more industrial land.

We now know that the theory of physical determinism is wrong.
The physical environment facilitates or enables personal relationships, but does not determine or shape them. (For a review of the
current state of the theory see Lee, 1971.) So physical planning, by
changing the physical environment cannot operate actively to make
desirable things happen: all that it can do is to operate passively
by inhibiting the conditions necessary for undesirable things or allowing the conditions necessary for desirable things.

As a result, town planners are now proposing other, non-physical,
means of tackling employment problems (see Palmer, 1975), and
architects are leaving community development to the Welfare and
Education Departments. But those changes are not before the theory
of physical determinism has produced its planning mistakes. In particular, many thousands of families are now living on public housing
estates which were intended as a means of social engineering, were
designed to create good neighbours and model citizens, and instead
have produced, at the extreme, vandalised estates which are shunned
by all but the most desperate.

INDEX TO REFERENCES IN CHAPTER 2

CAMERON, G. C. and JOHNSON, K. M., 1969, "Comprehensive urban renewal and indus-
    trial relocation", in Cullingworth, J. B. and Orr, S. C. (eds.), *Regional and Urban
    Studies*, Allen & Unwin, London.
CROSBY, T., 1965, *Architecture: City Sense*, Studio Vista, London.
DAVIES, J. G., 1972, *The Evangelistic Bureaucrat*, Tavistock Publications, London.
DENNIS, N., 1972, *Public Participation and Planning Blight*, Faber & Faber, London.
EVERSLEY, D. E. C., 1972, "Rising costs and static incomes", *Urban Studies*, vol. 9,
    no. 3.
Greater London Development Plan: "Statement", 1969, Greater London Council.
IAS/LA/4, 1975, "Labour Market Study", Department of the Environment, London.
IAS/LA/6, 1975, "Housing Stress", Department of the Environment, London.
IAS/LA/7, 1975, "Policies and Structure", Department of the Environment, London.
JACOBS, J., 1965, *The Death and Life of Great American Cities*, Penguin, Harmonds-
    worth.
KUPER, L. (ed.), 1953, *Living in Towns*, Cresset Press, London.

LEE, T., 1971, "The effects of the built environment on human behaviour", *International Journal of Environmental Studies*, vol. 1, no. 4.

NEWMAN, O., 1972, *Defensible Space*, Architectural Press, London.

PALMER, D. J., 1975, "Planning and forecasting employment and economic development in structure planning", *PRAG Technical Papers* 13, Centre for Environmental Studies, London.

CHAPTER 3

Flows of People

INTRODUCTION

"We have grown accustomed over the centuries", says Derek Senior (Royal Commission on Local Government, Vol. II, 1964), "to think of our social geography in terms of two contrasting elements. One is a continuous rural community, formed by scattered farmsteads and the hamlets, villages and small market towns within walking or riding distance of them. The other, punctuating this continuum, is a series of isolated, self-contained urban communities—industrial towns, cities and latterly conurbations...That is why...for thousands of years it made sense to use the same word, 'city', to denote both the *social unit* made up of the people who sustained and enjoyed the opportunities afforded by a city centre and the *built-up area* in which they had to live in order to do so. Geographically, the two things were co-terminous." But the motorcar has changed all that. Now the social unit, the area served by a city, is much larger than the physical unit of the built-up area: the social unit is now the *city region* of the built-up area plus the city's rural hinterland. (These geographical areas are represented in Fig. 3.1.)

In Chapters 3 and 4 we shall study interactions between two geographical areas within the city region—the bricks-and-mortar city and the rural hinterland. Why, when our guiding principle is the desire to understand how cities work, do we study also the rural hinterland? Because we cannot understand how the city—the bricks-and-mortar city—works without considering some of its interactions with its rural hinterland. In these two chapters we shall try to substantiate that answer.

(By a fortunate accident we are able to study these interactions using statistics collected for pre–1974 local authority areas. Those administrative boundaries of towns and cities are very similar to the ones drawn in 1888 when the system was started. Since 1888 the city as a social unit has spread far outside those boundaries,

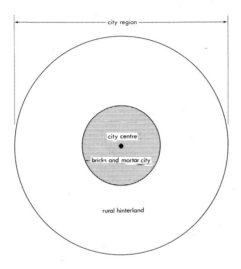

Fig. 3.1. Some geographical components of a city region.

but the city as a physical unit had remained, in most cases, within them. So it is that the pre–1974 distinction between urban administrative areas and rural administrative areas can in most cases be used to distinguish between the bricks-and-mortar city and the rural hinterland.)

That these interactions exist, are important, and are growing in importance is well-known and well documented: volume III of the report of the Royal Commission on Local Government in England (1969) investigated many of them, and its findings are used widely in these two chapters. It is not surprising that the old local authority system (changed in 1974) ignored them (with, for example, administratively independent county boroughs set in the midst of rural counties) for, as we have noted, that system dated from the nineteenth century. What is surprising is that in many cases the new local authority system also ignores the interactions: the metropolitan counties (e.g. the West Midlands County) have their boundaries drawn very tightly around the bricks-and-mortar conurbations, so that the built-up area is administered by one council, the rural hinterland by another.

The study of these interactions between a city and its hinterland will be divided between Chapters 3 and 4 as follows. In Chapter 3 we shall study the regular and recurrent *flows of people* between the two areas. In Chapter 4 we shall study how the rural hinterland is used as "Lebensraum" by a city, the residents of which press tightly on its space and resources. The rural hinterland is used as an overspill receptacle: the actions are one-way migrations from the city to the hinterland. (In other ways too the hinterland acts as an overspill receptacle for the city—e.g. for public utilities such as sewage works and refuse disposal—but we will not consider those here.) The title of Chapter 4, *Floods and overspills*, is a reference to Self's book *Cities in Flood* (1957) in which he describes the expansionary pressures within cities.

FLOWS OF PEOPLE INTO THE TOWN FOR SERVICES

Services, such as those provided by shops, banks, cinemas, have two properties which together explain why rural people have to travel into the town to use them. One property is that the services cannot be transported, so people have to travel to where the services are produced (e.g. the shop, the concert hall). The other property is that most services can be provided more efficiently on a large scale than a small scale so services are provided in just a few centres (e.g. a furniture shop in a village is not profitable). As a result, if you live in a village and want to buy a suit or arrange an over-draft you have to travel to the nearest town. That is not new: "to market, to market to buy a fat pig" has described journeys ever since households broke out of subsistence farming.

In this chapter we want to explain not why such journeys are made, but the nature of the journeys and the directions in which they are made. And for this explanation we use some parts of central place theory. (Other parts of central place theory are used, and other aspects of the interaction between people and services are described, in Chapter 7.)

In order to understand the nature and direction of the journeys that people make into cities to buy services it is necessary to use only one part of central place theory—the prediction that if central

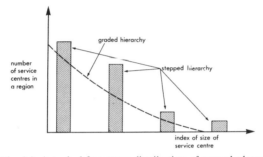

Fig. 3.2. A typical frequency distribution of central places.

places are graded by the number of service functions they perform, and a frequency distribution plotted of the number of places in each size class, then central places form a "stepped" hierarchy, not a "graded" hierarchy (see Fig. 3.2). (Alternatively, they form a "discrete" rather than a "continuous" stratification: Carter, 1972.) What that means is that central places can be put into discrete classes with real and big differences in size between each class. This prediction has been extensively tested and, in large measure, corroborated (see, for example, Shankland, Cox & Associates, 1966, append. D). What it means "on the ground" is shown for one region—Wales—in Fig. 3.3.

That might seem to be a pretty recondite, not to say useless, statement. Why make it? Its use is that from it can be deduced the following. In the competition between service centres for the trade of the

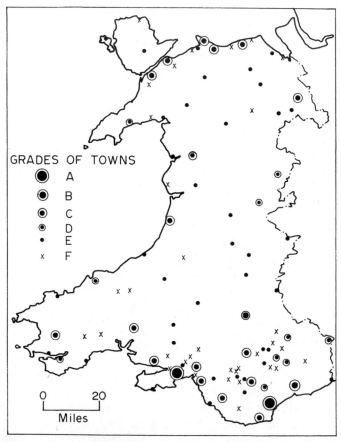

GRADES OF TOWNS

● A
◉ B
◉ C
◉ D
· E
× F

0   20

Miles

Fig. 3.3. Central places in Wales (from Carter, 1965, *Towns of Wales*, by courtesy of the University of Wales Press).

people who live around the centres, we know that service centres are unequal competitors: the biggest centres can compete with the smallest centres to sell loaves of bread, but the smallest centres cannot join in the competition to sell the services of a first division football team. Central place theory puts that observation on a systematic basis by predicting discrete classes of service centres (classified in terms of the number of functions which a centre can offer).

From that we can deduce that service *trade* too can be divided into discrete classes, and that there will be a hierarchy of *catchment areas* around centres, one for each class of trade.

So, if we call the highest class of centre grade A, there will be a part of the total service trade, class I trade, for which only grade A centres can compete, and around each grade A centre will be a catchment area enclosing those people who buy their class I trade in that centre. Class II trade is that part of the total trade for which centres of grades A and B, and grades A and B only, compete with each other: so around every grade A centre and grade B centre is a catchment area enclosing class II trade.

How do we use this to understand the nature and directions of the journeys which people make into cities to use services? Let us illustrate with the case in South Wales, as this has been carefully studied by Carter (1965, chap. 6). Cardiff is a "major city", which can compete with any other city in Britain except London. As a major city, Cardiff's nearest competitors are Birmingham, Liverpool and Bristol, so Cardiff's catchment area for this class of trade is formed by reference to those other major cities. The next important grade of centre is called by Carter a "major town": in that grade Cardiff's competitors are Swansea and Newport, and the catchment area around Cardiff for that class of trade is divided between those three major towns. Next come "regional centres", where Barry, Bridgend, and Pontypridd join Swansea and Newport in the competition against Cardiff: the resulting catchment area around Cardiff is smaller. And so we could go on, considering Cardiff as a "local centre", etc. (but in Chapter 7 we question whether central place theory should be used at such a small scale). The catchment areas are shown in Fig. 3.4 (which shows the predicted catchment areas. Some actual catchment areas are measured by Carter (pp. 112–15). They are similar to the predicted areas, but more complex.)

Another way of looking at these flows of people is to consider a household at, for example, Porthcawl (see Fig. 3.4). For groceries, that household will visit Porthcawl, for "regional centre" trade Bridgend, for "major town" trade Swansea, for "major city" trade Cardiff; and for presenting a petition against closing the local steel works that household will have to visit London.

How has this digression into central place theory helped us to understand the way in which cities provide services for their rural hinterlands? It has pointed out that the places from which people travel into the city for services depend, in a systematic way, on the nature of the services which they want and on the location of competing centres. Hence, a city has not one but a number of catchment

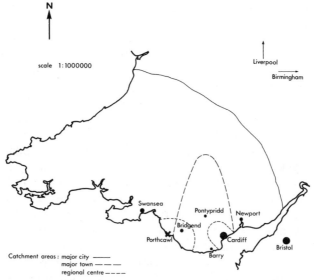

Fig. 3.4. Catchment areas around Cardiff.

areas from which it attracts custom. And as a corollary, when a city is acting as a service centre it has not one but a number of rural hinterlands.

FLOWS OF PEOPLE INTO THE TOWN FOR WORK

Just as it is not new that people travel into a town for its market, so it is not new that people travel into a town for its jobs. What is important to us is not the existence of these journeys-to-work flows but their increasing size and importance. The increase can be shown in a number of ways.

First, rural districts are becoming more dependent on towns for employment: in 1921, 14% of working people who lived in rural districts worked in urban areas, in 1966 that had increased to 37% (Royal Commission, 1969, Vol. III, table 6). At the same time, the employment centres are becoming more dependent on workers living elsewhere (Royal Commission 1969, Vol. III, map 14).

Neither of those two statements tells us anything about the origin of the work journeys into urban areas: do they come from the *adjacent* rural areas? To answer that we need to study the *commuting hinterlands* around cities. The Royal Commission report defines a "tight" commuting hinterland as enclosing all those local authority areas from which at least 500 workers travel to the employment centre, and a "loose" commuting hinterland enclosing areas which each contribute at least 100 workers to the centre. Using those concepts, the report investigates directly the changes in work journeys from rural hinterlands into cities. And what does it find? It finds that commuting hinterlands have increased in size, that people are making longer work journeys into cities. And it finds that employment centres are becoming more dependent on their commuting hinterlands to supply them with labour (Royal Commission, 1969, Vol. III, map 13 and p. 27, shows those findings for Coventry, Leicester and Northampton).

What are the reasons for the increasing size and importance of such work flows? One reason is that jobs in urban areas have been increasing faster than jobs in rural areas (e.g. agricultural employment has shrunk, service employment has grown and needs to be in towns and cities), while the population of rural areas has been increasing faster than the population of urban areas (see Chapter 4). The resulting geographical imbalance in labour supply and labour demand is removed by journeys-to-work (see Chapter 6) from rural areas into towns and cities. Such journeys have been made possible by increased personal mobility endowed by the growth of car-ownership, especially in rural areas. (Whereas in 1945 there were about 1,500,000 private cars and vans in Britain, in 1967 there were more than 10,000,000. And in 1966 there were 0.48 cars per household in urban areas but 0.72 in rural districts (Royal Commission, 1969, Vol. III, pp. 21, 22). It is an interesting question whether the higher car-ownership in rural areas is a *cause* of the longer work journeys into cities, or an *effect!*)

Who are the people who commute into the city from its rural hinterland? Are they different from the other workers in the city, those who live there as well as work there? The Royal Commission (1969, Vol. III, append. 3,) tried to answer that question by studying fourteen major employment centres in England, towns and cities which were free-standing and away from other cities and conurbations. "In every instance but one, the proportion of professional and managerial people among the incoming commuters is higher than among the centre's resident population. Taking the centres collectively the proportions are in round terms, $9\frac{1}{2}\%$ for the resident population of the centres and 16% for the commuters" (p. 46).

Why is there a difference in occupational composition? One reason is described more fully in Chapter 4: professional and managerial workers have been migrating out of the towns into rural areas faster than other occupational types. Another reason, no doubt related, is that such workers usually earn more money, and hence can better afford to commute. Another reason is that manual workers often work hours which are long and awkward, so they do not want long journeys in addition: imagine travelling for an hour before starting the 06.30 hour shift!

FLOWS OF PEOPLE OUT OF THE TOWNS FOR RECREATION

In an ingenious article, Cracknell (1967) describes the relationship between the city and its neighbouring countryside in the following terms. "The surrounding countryside is now being used as an extension of life in the city: it is the garden for the children to play in, a vista people can enjoy from their mobile room (i.e. their car).... For every city-dweller it has become, through the motor car, an integral part of his environment—it is part of the subconscious contract he makes with city living, namely that whenever he wants to, he can get out and enjoy the countryside. In a very real sense, the belt of countryside around a city has become its 'living space'."

That is a very imaginative way of describing how city residents use the surrounding rural hinterland for recreation. What is the evidence for it? The evidence is unsystematic and inconclusive, but Cracknell cites the following. A British survey in 1963 showed that more than half of the population did some pleasure travelling over the three-day Whit weekend and of those 60% travelled by car. Use of the car is not increasing the distance travelled on these trips, but is increasing the frequency of the trips by making them easier. A 1965 survey showed that the average distance travelled was 50 miles one-way on full-day trips and 28 miles one-way on half-day trips. Motorists visiting common lands on a Sunday were found to have travelled 12 miles on average. People living in a city drive into the countryside which is nearest to them: that is, they travel outwards from the centre, remaining in their "sector" of the city region. When people set out on one of these trips they often have no destination in mind: they are just going for a drive in the country. When they pull off the road for a stop, most people do not do very much, and do not move very far from the car: the countryside is treated as a garden at the end of a 30 minute car journey.

We can add some more survey evidence. Elson (1974) made a survey of pleasure trips into the country by car by households in Lewes, Sussex. He found that, in the summer, 73% of households made at least one trip every three Sundays, and that, throughout the year, 42% went once a fortnight, 20% once a week. And a survey of weekend motorists in the Lake District (Countryside Commission, undated, survey made in 1966) found "the furthest one-way journey distance for which a significant number of visitors is recorded is about 75 miles for day trips and 25 miles for half-day trips. This suggests that...motorists are prepared to travel for only $2-2\frac{1}{2}$ hours each way on day trips and less than 1 hour each way on half-day trips" (p. 24).

There are two further items of evidence which are consistent with the thesis that "the belt of countryside around a city has become its living space", and they are even more indirect. One is the congestion in the countryside around towns and cities on weekends, bank holidays, and fine summer evenings. The presumption is that most of the crowding is caused by people from the adjacent city. Another item is the difference in traffic flows on radial routes out of cities between the average weekday (two rush-hour peaks) and Sunday (a minor peak at 11.00 hours and a major peak from 18.00 to 21.00 hours) (see Cracknell, 1967, fig. 1).

Is it possible to measure the size of the *recreational hinterlands* around cities? Elson (1974) suggests that most recreation trips from a large town are contained within 30 miles of the town: but the total evidence is scanty. (Cracknell, 1967, does not measure the size of recreational hinterlands but predicts, with great ingenuity, how big they should be to accommodate all the casual car-trips by city dwellers.)

SOME FINANCIAL EFFECTS OF THESE FLOWS

The major interactions between a town and its rural hinterland, interactions which are regular and recurrent, we have described as: flows of people into the town for services, flows of people into the town for jobs, and flows of people out of the town for recreation. The first set of flows gives rise to not one, but several *service catchment areas*, the second to a *commuting hinterland*, the third to a *recreational hinterland*. So our simple view of the city region has to be qualified: there is not one rural hinterland around the built-up city but several. Hence there is no single definition of the city region.

Nevertheless, it remains that there are important and substantial interactions across the boundary of the built-up city and, in particular where the built-up city is separate administratively from its hinterland, the interactions can have important financial effects.

When people go into the town for *services*, they carry with them money which they spend in the town's shops and offices (the amounts of money carried can be estimated—see Chapter 7). That increases the incomes of the service workers who work in the town, it increases the money demand for maintaining and constructing buildings in the town, and it increases the rateable value of the town. All that financial gain to the town is financial loss to the rural hinterland. But at the same time, visitors to the town create a demand for services which must be provided by the local authority, at the expense of the town's ratepayers (e.g. public transport, street cleaning, car parks—see the argument applied to London in Chapter 2).

The commuters who travel into the town for *work* require very expensive transport facilities—roads, public transport, car parks, etc.—and the greatest expense is in the town not in the rural areas. Insofar as the expense is paid by the city council (some is paid by central government and some by the users) it is a cost on city residents to provide for rural residents. On the other hand, the shops, offices and factories in the cities to which the outsiders commute are very valuable and pay high rates. That is a great financial gain to the city. (When the implications of a road across the Dee estuary were being investigated, one strong possibility was that the new road would attract to Flintshire people who would work in Merseyside. That would have meant that Flintshire got new residents—who make heavier demands on the rates than they contribute—and little new industry—which contributes more to the rates than it takes away. So it was necessary to insist that the growth be not just of housing but also of industry. See Shankland, Cox & Associates, 1970, p. 53.)

It is widely believed that tourism is a moneyspinner, and therefore that families who travel out of the town for *recreation* bring financial gain to the rural hinterland. It is probable, however, that only certain types of recreational visit—mainly those involving overnight stays— are valuable to the residents of the place visited (see Archer and Owen, 1971; Brownrigg and Greig, 1976). Moreover, it is probable that day-trips and half-day trips are a financial liability to the place visited. The visitors spend very little money in the countryside, often buying all they need (petrol, picnic, drinks) in the town before leaving. And once in the country, car-borne visitors want facilities (such as roadside toilets, car parks, litter bins) which have to be provided by the local council. Moreover, the visitors from the city often cause damage, which costs the rural residents yet more money. So the financial effect of recreational trips from the city into the surrounding country is usually a loss to the latter: it is partly in recognition of this that, under the Countryside Act 1968, county boroughs may establish and pay for country parks in the areas of county councils. (Another effect of the Dee crossing might have been to increase the number of day-trippers from Merseyside into Flintshire and Denbighshire. So that report—Shankland, Cox & Associates, 1970, chap. 10—recommended a recreational strategy which aimed to extract the maximum money out of day-trippers and to cause minimum cost to Flintshire and Denbighshire.)

INDEX TO REFERENCES IN CHAPTER 3

ARCHER, B. H. and OWEN, C. B., 1971, "Towards a tourist regional multiplier", *Regional Studies*, vol. 5, no. 4.

BROWNRIGG, M. and GREIG, M., 1976, *Tourism on Skye*, Fraser of Allander Institute, Strathclyde University.

CARTER, H., 1965, *Towns of Wales*, University of Wales Press, Cardiff.

CARTER, H., 1972, *The Study of Urban Geography*, Arnold, London.

COUNTRYSIDE COMMISSION, undated, *Pleasure Traffic and Recreation in the Lake District*, Countryside Commission, London.

CRACKNELL, B., 1967, "Accessibility to the countryside as a factor in planning for leisure", *Regional Studies*, vol. 1, no. 2.

ELSON, M., 1974, "The weekend car", *New Society*, no. 601.

ROYAL COMMISSION ON LOCAL GOVERNMENT IN ENGLAND 1966–69, 1969, CMND 4040, HMSO, London.

SELF, P., 1957, *Cities in Flood*, Faber & Faber, London.

SHANKLAND, COX & ASSOCIATES, 1966, *Expansion of Ipswich*, HMSO, London.

SHANKLAND, COX & ASSOCIATES, 1970, *Deeside*, London.

FURTHER READING FOR CHAPTER 3

BERRY, B. J. L. and HORTON, F. E., 1970, *Geographic Perspectives on Urban Systems*, Prentice Hall, New Jersey, chapters 7, 8.

CARTER, H., 1972, *The Study of Urban Geography*, Arnold, London, chapters 4, 5, 6, 7.

DICKINSON, R. E., 1967, *The City Region in Western Europe*, Routledge & Kegan Paul, London, parts I and II.

JOHNSON, J. H., 1967, *Urban Geography*, Pergamon, Oxford, chapter 5.

JONES, E., 1966, *Towns and Cities*, OUP, London, chapters 5, 6.

ROYAL COMMISSION ON LOCAL GOVERNMENT IN ENGLAND, 1966–69, vol. III, 1969, HMSO, London.

SMAILES, A. E., 1966, *The Geography of Towns*, Hutchinson, London, chapter 7.

CHAPTER 4

Floods and Overspills

MIGRATION OUT OF THE TOWNS

In the last chapter we studied one set of interactions between the built-up city and its rural hinterland—the regular and recurrent two-way flows of people between the two geographical areas. The actions which we study in this chapter are the rural hinterland acting as a receptacle for the town's overspill population, the effect of that on the town especially when the action is distorted by green belts, and the effect on the social geography of the rural hinterland. So the flows which are the subject of this chapter are of people moving out of the town to live in the rural hinterland. Much of the evidence about the size and direction of these flows we take from the Royal Commission on Local Government (1969) (which was our source book for much of Chapter 3 also).

First we note that rural districts are gaining population relative to urban areas, the reverse of what happened in the last century: between 1891 and 1901 the population of urban areas grew by 19.9% and of rural areas fell by 7.9%, between 1961 and 1971 the population of urban areas grew by 2.4% and of rural areas by 18.0% (Hall *et al.*, 1973, Vol. I, p. 61). And we note that that is the result not just of rural areas growing more quickly than towns, but of many towns actually losing population (see Table 4.1). Moreover, it is the biggest cities which are losing population fastest: the biggest population losses are from the county boroughs at the centres of the conurbations, with Liverpool declining by 61,000 people (8% of its population), Manchester declining by 61,000 also (9%), Newcastle-upon-Tyne by 23,000 (8%), and Birmingham by a mere 8,000 (1%), all

TABLE 4.1. LOCAL AUTHORITIES WITH DECLINING POPULATIONS

	Proportion of local authorities with declining populations	
	1891–1901	1956–1966
County boroughs	3.1%	38.0%
Municipal boroughs	23.9%	17.0%
Urban districts	21.0%	13.9%
All urban	20.4%	17.3%
Rural districts	59.6%	17.5%
All authorities	35.0%	17.4%

Source: Royal Commission, 1969, p. 29.

between 1956 and 1966 (Royal Commission, 1969, p. 29). Expressed in terms of the city region (see Fig. 3.1), almost all towns are surrounded by rural hinterlands which are gaining people, and many of the towns are losing people.

What are the reasons for such changes in the distribution of England's population? The towns are losing people to the country for four main reasons: much of the old high-density housing in towns is being replaced with housing at lower densities; people are wanting to live in cleaner, quieter, greener areas (see, for example, Willmott and Young, 1957, chap. 8); people are wanting more space in and around the home; and households are containing fewer people yet still wanting separate dwellings. As a result, urban densities are falling (e.g. between 1901 and 1960 urban densities in England and Wales fell from 61 acres per 1000 people—40.6 persons per hectare—to 87 acres per 1000 people—28.4 persons per hectare. Royal Commission, 1969, p. 31, derived from Best and Coppock, 1962). So towns can accommodate fewer people, and the extra people move out across the town's boundaries. People are able to live in rural areas although jobs and services remain in the towns (see Chapter 3) because so many households now own cars.

So far we have talked about people moving out of towns and into rural hinterlands. But how many of the people who emigrate from a particular town settle in the rural hinterland of that town? In a special study of some Midland towns, the Royal Commission on Local Government (1969, map 16) found that in some cases up to 60% of all the people who left a town moved into the rural hinterland around it. Similarly, a high proportion of all the people who moved into a particular rural hinterland came from the town at its centre. "It is clear," says Hall (Hall *et al.*, 1973, Vol. II, p. 250) "that the biggest changes in population distribution (in England) are associated with centrifugal migration from the major urban concentrations rather than interregional moves."

Who are the people who migrate across a town's boundary in that way? Suspecting that towns were losing over their borders a disproportionate number of their vigorous and prosperous people, the Royal Commission (1969, append. 3) made a special study of fourteen county boroughs, all of them free-standing towns, away from conurbations and surrounded by countryside. Around each town a rural hinterland was drawn using information about the town's sphere of influence. Then, net migration between the town and its hinterland was studied, for the period 1961-6. Three population classes were defined—"working men" (males aged 15 and over), "prosperous men" (males aged 15 and over in professional and managerial socio-economic groups), and "vigorous men" (working males aged 25-44). For each of the fourteen towns, the direction of the net migration was from the town into its hinterland for each of the three population classes separately. And in almost every case, towns were losing higher proportions of their "prosperous men" and their "vigorous men" than their "working men". In other words, "prosperous" and "vigorous" men formed a higher proportion of the "working" men who migrated over a town's borders than of the "working" men who remained behind.

OVERSPILL, PLANNED AND UNPLANNED

The movement of people out of towns into their surrounding hinterlands is often given the name—ugly, mechanical, and unhuman though it is—of "overspill". In what kinds of vessels does the hinterland receive and accommodate the overspill that slops over the edges of the town? (That analogy shows the word "overspill" to be misleading: we have seen that people move out of towns not because the population has grown to a volume which the town cannot hold but because the volume which a town can comfortably hold is decreasing.) In particular, how much of the overspill is "planned" and how much "unplanned". *Planned* overspill is where the migrating households settle in new towns, town expansions, and satellite housing estates (e.g. Dagenham outside London, Chelmsley Wood outside Birmingham). The housing is built on a large scale for public or private tenure, and associated jobs, shops, schools, etc., are provided. The new development is built to a comprehensive plan and is implemented by special legislation (e.g. the New Towns Act 1965, the Town Development Act 1952). *Unplanned* overspill refers to all other overspill: usually the migrants settle into small private housing estates on the edges of villages or country towns. The only planning is the normal statutory planning—i.e. development control—of the receiving local authority.

In 1944 it was proposed that most of the overspill from London should be directed into planned communities: Abercrombie (1945) recommended that there should be a *net* migration out of the built-up area into the surrounding metropolitan region of 1,166,000 people, of whom no less than 952,000 should go into planned developments (see Table 4.2). What has actually happened? Between 1952 and 1958 there was a *gross* migration of 255,000 people out of the conurbation, less than half (175,000) into planned schemes (Powell, 1961—see Table 4.2). And between 1961 and 1966 there was a *net* migration from Greater London into the rest of the South East region of 414,000 people, of whom only 72,000 were net migration into planned schemes (Sample Census 1966—see Table 4.2). The absolute figures are not comparable: what can be said is that the proportion of London's overspill which is planned is very much lower than Abercrombie proposed. Cullingworth (1960) pointed out that in 1960: we have shown that plans are still not being achieved.

What are likely to be the relative proportions of planned and unplanned overspill in the future? Alas, we cannot say because the planners will not say! In 1964, when the planners were bolder (or more reckless), it was proposed that overspill from London into the South East Region should be 60% planned, 40% unplanned (i.e.

TABLE 4.2. DESTINATION OF OVERSPILL FROM LONDON

After 1945, proposed by Abercrombie net migration from London conurbation		1952–8, actual overspill gross migration from London conurbation		1961–6 actual net migration from Greater London	
quasi-satellites	125,000	LCC estates beyond conurbation	45,000		
new towns	383,000	8 London new towns	120,000	8 London new towns	37,000
planned town expansions up to 50 miles from London	425,000	town expansions	10,000	13 town expansions within S.E Region for London	
larger houses (i.e. private) in planned satellites	19,000				
total in planned schemes	952,000	total in planned schemes	175,000	total in planned schemes (excluding satellite estates)	72,000
"free choice" houses within the region	214,000	private moves to and beyond the green belt	180,000	other destinations within S.E. Region	342,000
total within region	1,166,000	total overspill	355,000	total within S.E. region	414,000
beyond the metropolitan influence	100,000			total to rest of G.B.	59,000

Sources: Abercrombie, 1945, chap. 3.   Powell, 1961.   Sample Census 1966.

people moving "under their own arrangements and who will need to be provided for in the ordinary land allocations of the local planning authorities"—*The South East Study*, 1964, p. 54). In 1967 the South East Economic Planning Council (1967, p. 14) changed that, implicitly, into a higher proportion of unplanned overspill. By 1970, the South East Joint Planning Team (1970, chap. 10) would make no proposals for how the overspill should be thus divided. Nor, in another region, would another regional planning team by 1971 (West Midlands Regional Study, 1971, chap. 5).

GREEN BELTS

The picture of the city region which we have been using so far (see Fig. 3.1) has ignored the green belts which encircle eighteen of our major cities. So we have been talking about interactions between the physical city and its rural hinterland without taking account of green belts. Is that acceptable, when two of the purposes for which green belts were established in 1955 are: to check the further growth of a large built-up area, and: to prevent neighbouring towns from merging into one another (Ministry of Housing, 1955)? Moreover, green belts cover a significant proportion of the land surface of England and Wales—9.7%, or 5709 square miles, for green belt submissions. And of these submissions, 2540 square miles have been formally approved (Gregory, 1970, p. 1, modified by green belt confirmations since 1970).

In defence of our omission so far you might say: but only three green belt proposals have been confirmed, around London, Oxford and Birmingham. But that is no defence: all green belt submissions are treated as *de facto* green belts even though not officially approved. Another defence might be: but population statistics show that the movement of people out of towns into the surrounding rural areas has not been stopped by green belts. True: but have green belts reduced that movement? We cannot avoid the questions: what has been the effect of green belts on the migration of people out of towns? If there have been some effects, what have been the consequences for the towns and for their rural hinterlands?

In one of the few empirical studies of green belts, Gregory (1970, p. 65) concludes for part of the West Midlands green belt, "... green belt policy has been extremely effective in restricting the physical expansion of the conurbation into (the immediate rural hinterland)". If we can generalise from that to all green belts, we can say that *short-distance* overspill (i.e. migration from the towns to just over their physical boundaries) has been reduced by green belts. If that is so, what effects would we expect to see on the towns and their hinterlands? Gregory (1972) suggests the following effects: unfortunately there is little empirical evidence to test his hypotheses.

People are still moving out of the physical city. But they have to jump across the immediate rural hinterland (the green belt) and live further out. As a result, such migratory moves are further than they would have been in the absence of green belts. So some people who might have left the city have to stay in the city instead. As a result, pressure on the physical city is greater than it would have been. That causes land within the city boundaries to be used more intensively: land prices are higher, housing densities on infill sites are higher, old lower density housing is redeveloped at higher densities, derelict land (often acting as recreational open space) is reclaimed and built upon, sports clubs sell their suburban sites for housing and buy bigger sites in the green belt, and so on. All those extra pressures tend to worsen living conditions within the city.

In the rural hinterland, the effect is selective immigration. If you live in the rural hinterland and work in the city, the effect of a green belt is to increase your commuting costs. That means that only the richer people can afford to move out of the cities, a trend reinforced by the worsening environmental conditions in cities (see above). The other effect of green belts on rural hinterlands is absurd: some towns and villages within the green belt find it difficult to get permission to build housing for their own natural growth, and may have to send their overspill beyond the green belt!

(It is unlikely that such effects were foreseen when green belts were introduced. So they can be added to the examples in Chapter 2 of bad planning caused by planners working in ignorance of a system of activities and spaces—in this case the system of people migrating out of towns.)

THE METROPOLITAN FRINGE

We need to look a little more closely at the rural hinterland of cities, especially of major cities and metropolitan areas for which the hinterland is sometimes called the "metropolitan fringe". The migration out of towns which we have been studying, a migration modified by green belts—what is it doing to the metropolitan fringe? We know that it is adding to the population of that area with planned and unplanned overspill, with owner-occupiers and public tenants, and that the migrants contain a higher proportion of prosperous and vigorous families than remain behind in the city. Is there anything more to be said?

There is for, according to Pahl (1970), what is developing in the metropolitan fringe is "a new form of dispersed city" (p. 20), an "area of constant heterogeneity with no gradient of density of development" (p. 30), a society which is rural physically but urban socially, an *urbs in rure.*

Pahl's first studies were in Hertfordshire (Pahl, 1965—later work was in Kent) an area of very rapid growth caused largely by migration from London. The migration has been into settlements both planned (the new towns of Stevenage and Welwyn Garden City) and unplanned (certain villages designated by planners for expansion). Most importantly, the migration has been accompanied by *segregation*. There is segregation within new towns; the residents redistribute themselves internally, creating rough districts and respectable districts. Many middle class people segregate themselves by deciding not to live in the new towns at all, but in fashionable parts of older towns or in the country. Within the rural areas some villages become fashionable and some not. The fashionable villages attract middle class people who live segregated from the established population even within the same village (see also Connell, 1971). Segregation is an urban characteristic, and it has been introduced into rural districts.

Another urban characteristic which migration has taken to the rural hinterland is commuting. "New towns are not self-contained and 'rural' areas are rapidly increasing in population. Commuting is not confined to the middle class, but the working class is more limited by transport" (Pahl, 1965, p. 72).

So the migration from the cities is causing the old hierarchies in the cities' rural hinterland to collapse. The social hierarchy is collapsing as segregation leads to the polarisation of the social structure along class lines. And the geographical hierarchy is collapsing as people segregate, migrate selectively, commute: towns take on specialist functions "so that they might be better understood as interlocking parts of a dispersed city." (Pahl, 1965, p. 72).

The rural hinterland succumbs to the invasion from the city.

SOME FINANCIAL EFFECTS

Migration of people from cities into their hinterlands has some important financial effects on the two geographical areas. For example, the city still has to provide for workers within its boundaries although many of those workers now live beyond the boundaries: if there is unemployment among the city residents, and the city spends money stimulating the provision of more jobs, those jobs might be taken by inward commuters. Also, there is an increase in the ratio of a city's necessary expenditure to its residents who pay for the expenditure (see the example of London in Chapter 2). Moreover, it is the richer residents who move out, so the greater expenditure per resident has to be borne by poorer people. The journey-to-work flows from the hinterland into the city have additional financial effects which were described in Chapter 3: green belts increase those effects.

INDEX TO REFERENCES IN CHAPTER 4

ABERCROMBIE, P., 1945, *Greater London Plan, 1944*, HMSO, London.

BEST, R. H. and COPPOCK, J. T., 1962, *The Changing Use of Land in Britain*, Faber & Faber, London.

CONNELL, J., 1971, "Green belt country", *New Society* no. 439.

CULLINGWORTH, J. B., 1960, *Housing Needs and Planning Policy*, Routledge & Kegan Paul, London.

GREGORY, D. G., 1970, *Green Belts and Development Control*, CURS occasional papers no. 12, Birmingham.

GREGORY, D. G., 1972, "Observations on the proposed West Midlands green belt", paper given to the Regional Studies Association and the Royal Town Planning Institute, Birmingham.

HALL, P. *et al.*, 1973, *The Containment of Urban England*, Allen & Unwin, London.

MINISTRY OF HOUSING, 1955, *Green Belts* circular 42/55, HMSO, London.

PAHL, R. E., 1965, *Urbs in Rure*, LSE geographical papers no. 2, London.

PAHL, R. E., 1970, *Whose City?* Longman, London.

POWELL, A. G., 1961, "The recent development of Greater London", *The Advancement of Science*, vol. 17.

Royal Commission on Local Government in England 1966–69, 1969, vol. III, CMND 4040, HMSO, London.

Sample Census 1966, Migration Summary table, part I, and Migration regional report, S.E. region, HMSO, London.

South East Economic Planning Council, 1967, *A Strategy for the South East*, HMSO, London.

South East Joint Planning Team, 1970, *Strategic Plan for the South East*, HMSO, London.

The South East Study, 1964, HMSO, London.

West Midlands Regional Study, 1971, *A Developing Strategy for the West Midlands*, Birmingham.

WILLMOTT, P. and YOUNG, M., 1957, *Family and Kinship in East London*, Routledge & Kegan Paul, London.

FURTHER READING FOR CHAPTER 4

CARTER, H., 1972, *The Study of Urban Geography*, Arnold, London, chapter 12.

CULLINGWORTH, J. B., 1960, *Housing Needs and Planning Policy*, Routledge & Kegan Paul, London.

DICKINSON, R. E., 1967, *The City Region in Western Europe*, Routledge & Kegan Paul, London, parts I and II.

HALL, P. *et al.*, 1973, *The Containment of Urban England*, Allen & Unwin, London.

JONES, E., 1966, *Towns and Cities*, OUP, London, chapter 6.

PAHL, R., 1975, *Whose City?*, Penguin, Harmondsworth, parts 1 and 2.

Royal Commission on Local Government in England, 1966–69, vol. III, 1969, HMSO, London.

SELF, P., 1957, *Cities in Flood*, Faber, London.

CHAPTER 5

People and Housing

THE SUPPLY AND DEMAND APPROACH

This chapter and the two that follow it are about the interactions between people and facilities within a town, and the same general method can fruitfully be used to study all the three sets of interactions. The method can be described as follows:

people want to use facilities;
facilities have to be provided by someone;
there are connections between the decision to provide the facility and the desire to use the facility (e.g. the provision is in response to the desire to use, or the availability of a facility stimulates the desire to use it).

This method of analysis can conveniently be called the "supply and demand approach". People *demand* a facility. The facility is *supplied*. Supply and demand interact in the *market* for that facility, and as a result there is a certain level of *provision* and *use* of the facility.

However, that terminology, although convenient, is also dangerous, for our rather lax use of the words "supply", "demand", and "market" might be confused with the much more precise use of those words in economics. In economics "demand" means the amount demanded at a given price, "supply" means the amount supplied at a given price, and in the "market" supply and demand interact to set a price which determines both the level of provision and of use. Such precise economic analysis can be used to study the interactions between people and those facilities which are commercially provided (e.g. commercial services, private housing). But many urban facilities are not commercially provided (e.g. education, outdoor recreation). For such facilities, the supply and demand approach can be very usefully applied, as long as we do not give to that approach the meaning which it has in economic theory.

HOUSING AS A PUBLIC AND A PRIVATE CONCERN

To a family, housing is a private concern. Moreover, shelter is a basic human need, and housing has come to have great social and economic significance. So housing is a very great private concern to a family, and families express that concern by being prepared to pay a high proportion of their incomes to secure housing. In many countries (and in particular in Britain) governments are keenly interested in how well their citizens are housed. The quality of housing affects the ability of people to work, and affects public health. Moreover, there is compassion in government interest in housing: it is a social and political issue if some citizens are badly housed. So housing is a public concern also.

A useful way of distinguishing between the private view and the public view of housing is to distinguish between the *economic demand* for housing and the *need* for housing.

The economic demand for housing expresses the private view: it describes the amount of housing which private households are prepared to buy (in a given period of time) when a unit of housing has a given price. The relationship between amount demanded and unit price is the demand schedule. For example, if the price of three-bedroom semi-detached houses in good condition and centrally heated in Birmingham were £1000, then the number of such houses that people would be prepared to buy in a year would be X1: if the price were £2000, X2 would be demanded: if the price were £3000, X3 would be demanded: and so on.

The need for housing at one time is a measure of the number of families who are inadequately housed: it is calculated by comparing the conditions in which people are actually housed with the minimum conditions in which it is thought that people should be housed. Those minimum conditions are housing standards which are set by a public body, so housing need is the public view of housing. Housing standards include a value judgement which, if the measure of housing need is to be used to improve housing conditions irrespective of households' abilities to pay, must be publicly accepted. (In the terms of Bradshaw, 1972, housing need is a "normative need".) A related meaning of "housing need" is the number of dwellings that will be needed by some time in the future if the present deficiency is to be made up and all future households are to be accommodated to the minimum standard (whether or not those future households could secure for themselves adequate housing. See, for example, Watson *et al.*, 1973).

So housing demand is a positive (non-normative) concept, related to an impersonal, amoral housing market. Housing need is a normative concept, related to social values and not to price or ability to pay. That distinction must always be carefully made: some examples will show why.

If council house rents were not subsidised, if there were no rent rebates, and if rents were set "in the market", the housing list of people wanting council houses would automatically disappear: a price would result at which there would be no unsatisfied demand. But there would still be housing need.

By setting housing standards very low, you can define housing need out of existence; there is very little housing need in Britain if the minimum standard is that everyone should have a roof over his head. Alternatively, by setting housing standards very high, you can say that Buckingham Palace is a slum; or you can require that new private housing be built to such high standards that no-one can afford to buy it, when there will be no housing demand for it (see, for example, *Housing in the North West Region* 1970, for the argument that there is not a big demand for private houses built up to the Parker Morris standards of local authority housing); or you can require a housing programme to meet the housing need so great that it would absorb all the country's productive capacity.

"The major interest in post-war Britain has been housing need" says Cullingworth (1969, p. 150). That has two important consequences for the study of housing in Britain, consequences which we must remember always. The first consequence is that the government has intervened in the housing market to a massive extent, and so has "distorted" (to use the value-laden terminology of *laissez-faire* economic theory) the market. So serious anomalies have arisen, such as reported by the Milner Holland Report (MHLG, 1965) which showed that the weekly net cost to the occupier of a house costing £3750 including land could range from £2.35 to £7.07, depending on the form of tenure. Another example of "distortion" is the absence of financial inducements to private landlords and the presence of financial inducement to all other house owners, which is contributing to the disappearance of private dwellings for rent.

The second consequence of the British emphasis on housing need is that most housing data collected in Britain are about need and not demand. So the definitions of households and dwellings are in physical terms, not in terms of money (see below), as are the data to measure unfit housing or over-crowding. And there are very few surveys of what people actually want in housing and how much they are prepared to pay for it. As Cullingworth says (1969, p. 186) "It is likely that increasing interest will be focussed on consumer preference and economic demand. Major changes in housing policy will, however, be needed before it is possible to examine market forces as distinct from attitudes."

HOUSEHOLDS AND DWELLINGS

In what units is housing to be studied? The British convention is to say that a *household* demands housing, and that housing is supplied as *dwellings*. It is necessary to understand precisely what those terms mean.

A *household* is a group of people who live together. Thus, the Census 1971 (p. 5) says, "A household is either one person living alone or a group of persons (who may or may not be related) living at the same address with common housekeeping." (Note that a household may not be the same as a family.) Not everyone lives in households: a few people live in "non-private establishments", such as hotels, colleges, prisons.

Dwellings are usually defined in terms of structurally separate accommodation. For the great majority of dwellings that presents no difficulties; detached, semi-detached, and terraced houses, and flats in purpose-built blocks are easily recognisable as separate structures. The difficulties arise when two or more separate households share some or all of their household spaces. In such cases the Census 1971 (p. 7) defines dwellings as follows; where the shared space is for access only, the space occupied by each household is a separate dwelling; where the shared space is for other uses (e.g. cooking, moving between rooms), the space occupied by all the households is one dwelling (so the dwelling is shared by two or more households).

On those definitions, we can compare the number of dwellings and of households: that is done for England and Wales in Table 5.1, and we find more dwellings available than there are households. (The calculation cannot be made for 1971, as that Census did not count vacant dwellings.) So there is no housing shortage in Britain!

The simple comparison leads to a false conclusion for at least seven reasons. It does not allow for the households which use more than one dwelling (e.g. families with second homes in the countryside); it does not allow for some dwellings to be empty while households move from one dwelling to another (indeed, it is necessary to have a small proportion of excess dwellings—2% or 3%— to facilitate such movements); it does not allow for households wanting dwellings in one area—e.g. Birmingham—when the spare dwellings are available elsewhere—e.g. mid–Wales; it does not allow for some of the available dwellings being unfit for habitation; it does not allow for some households to be sharing dwellings; it does not allow for the so-called "suppressed" households; and it does not allow for some dwellings not being available to households because of price and tenure. Let us look at the last three points.

A rough adjustment can be quickly made for those households sharing dwellings (see Table 5.1). To allow for suppressed households is much more difficult: we shall explain. A group of people may be living together as one household when, if housing were easier to obtain, they would try to split up into more households (the process known as household "fission"). It is said that such fissile households contain "suppressed" households. For example, between 1961

TABLE 5.1. POPULATION, HOUSEHOLDS AND DWELLINGS IN ENGLAND AND WALES

	1961	1966	1971
population	46,105,000	47,136,000	48,594,000
dwellings, occupied and vacant	14,646,000	15,449,000	16,455,000
households, present	14,641,000	15,360,000	16,510,000
excess of dwellings over households	5,000	89,000	
number of shared dwellings	350,000	442,000	271,000
number of households sharing dwellings	886,000	1,116,000	673,000
extra dwellings to eliminate sharing	536,000	674,000	366,000
shortage of dwellings	531,000	585,000	

Sources: Census of England and Wales, 1961, Housing Tables, HMSO, London. Sample Census, England and Wales, 1966, Housing Tables, HMSO, London. Census 1971, England and Wales, Housing, parts I, II, III, HMSO, London.

Notes: Only occupied dwellings were counted for 1971. It is dangerous to make comparisons between 1961, 1966 and 1971 values, because some definitions change between censuses. In particular, dwellings were defined differently in 1971 than earlier.

and 1971 in England and Wales, the population increased by 6.4% but the number of households increased by 12.8% (see Table 5.1). Part of the reason for the extra households was changing demographic structure (e.g. a greater proportion of old persons creating small households), but part was household fission as suppressed households became able to afford to set up home separately (e.g. newly-weds could afford to choose not to live with their in-laws).

Cullingworth (1969, p. 160) investigates suppressed households by using the concept of a "household unit"—a group of people who would, probably, like to live together as a separate household if they could obtain a dwelling. That concept, therefore, can be used to refine our measure of housing need. Cullingworth estimates that there were 15,043,000 household units in England and Wales in 1961. The crude excess of dwellings over households of 5000 (Table 5.1) thus becomes an excess of household units over dwellings of 397,000. (But note that that is a measure of housing need, not of housing demand.) A similar concept is of "potential households", defined as families and other groups likely to want separate dwellings. Their number is estimated as "the total of census type households *plus* married couple families, with or without children, not forming or heading a household, *less* three quarters of those one-person households who share dwellings with other households" (Housing Statistics, 1969).

Estimates of housing need are usually based on the standard of a separate dwelling for every household that wants one. The value of the concepts of household units and potential households is that either can be used to estimate the number of households into which a given population, specified by age, sex and marital status, would divide if there were no suppressed households. (Estimates of potential households use the method of headship rates: for examples of applications see Watson, 1973, and Shankland, Cox & Associates, 1968, append. B.) The alternative method of estimating housing needs which planners sometimes use is to divide a population total by an assumed average household size: that method, however, takes no account of the demographic composition of the population.

The point about price and tenure of dwellings is about how dwellings are allocated to households. Dwellings can be held (i.e. their "tenure") by their occupiers (owner-occupiers), by a local authority or new town development corporation renting to tenants, or by a private landlord renting to tenants. A household may want to buy a dwelling, but not qualify for a mortgage; or it may want to rent from the council but not qualify even to get on the housing list. So it cannot be assumed that dwellings in general will be allocated to households in general; it is necessary to know what types of dwellings and what types of households (see, for example, Crofton and Webster, 1974).

HOUSING DEMAND AND HOUSING SUPPLY

The relationship between the demand for housing and its supply is very complex. In particular, our discussion of suppressed households brings to our notice that demand is not independent of supply, that the number of households into which a given population divides depends upon the availability of dwellings. For example, if housing is tight and incomes are low, a group of students may share a flat and constitute one household; if housing is easier the group may split up and form several single person households. Or consider old people, numerically very important in the population; they may want to live on their own (separate households) or with their children (joint households), or in old people's dwellings (non-private establishments). Or consider older teenagers; they may live with parents or, if housing is more easily available, get a separate flat. Also, our discussion of housing allocation shows us that we must talk about the tenure groups separately. So in this section we can do no more than describe the supply of, and demand for housing (using those terms in the loose sense described earlier) in general terms.

DEMAND

If I want to buy a house, then I express my demand in terms of a willingness to pay for a particular type of house. The size of my demand is measured by how much I offer. But houses cost a lot of money, and it is unlikely that I will have the cash to buy the house outright: so I will want to borrow the cash. Fortunately, as well as costing a lot, houses last a long time, so a house is a good security on which to borrow money over a long time. That means that I will want to borrow money to buy a house, and that I will be able to do so: there are various financial institutions which lend money for housing. However, the dependence on borrowing money means that the lending institutions can have a big influence on the effective demand for housing. For example, if they have no money to lend, demand to buy will drop: if they have much money to lend, demand to buy will rise (and so, in the short run, may house prices). And if, for example, the lending institutions regard single people as a bad risk, such people will be unable to borrow money so their demand to buy houses will be small.

If I want to rent a private dwelling, then again I express my demand by being willing to pay. The size of my demand is measured by how much rent I am prepared to offer.

If I want to rent a public dwelling (e.g. from a local authority or a new town development corporation), then I express my demand by filling in a form applying to be put on the housing list. I might try to express the size of my demand by banging on the housing manager's desk: but the effective size of my demand is calculated by the housing authority which gives me points for length of residence, size of family, present housing conditions, etc. I may offer to pay more rent, but that has no effect on the size of my demand.

There are in Britain other ways of demanding housing, but they are not numerically very important—e.g. through housing associations, housing societies, tied housing (e.g. you can demand the vicarage by getting appointed as vicar).

SUPPLY

We tend to think of the supply of housing in terms of the construction of new houses, public housing and private housing. But it is important to remember that new housing adds usually less than 2% per annum to the total stock of dwellings in the United Kingdom (*Social Trends* 1975. New construction 1973–4, 278,000 dwellings; stock at end of 1974, 20,095,000 dwellings.) The reason for that is, of course, the extreme longevity of houses. Moreover, "less than one quarter of the households who move each year move into newly built houses. All except 'new' households (i.e. those who previously lived as part of other households or in individual accommodation...) move from houses in the existing stock. The character of the existing stock—as well as its overall size—thus appears to be of greater significance in the "supply' of housing than new house building." (Cullingworth, 1969, p. 153.) So most supply is from the existing housing stock (Table 5.2).

When private existing housing is offered for sale, the supply is by the existing owner. He supplies in response to the offer of money.

TABLE 5.2. STOCK OF DWELLINGS AT THE END OF 1974 (U.K.)

Owner-occupied	10,536,000
Rented from local authority or New Town Corporation	6,228,000
Rented from private owners, and other tenures	3,331,000
Total	20,095,000

Social Trends, No. 6, 1975, HMSO, London.

And often he needs that money from the sale in order to make effective his demand for another house. When private existing housing is supplied for rent, the supply is by the owner (or by the previous lessee if he assigns the lease). Again, the supply is in response to the offer of money.

When public existing housing is supplied for rent, the supply is by the owner (e.g. the local authority) offering a vacant property (a "re-let") or by the previous tenant (doing a swop with another tenant). The owner supplies in response to a statutory obligation created by social and political decisions. The previous tenant supplies in response to a desire to get a more suitable dwelling.

That small part of the supply of housing which comes from new construction is supplied partly by the public and partly by the private sector: of the 364,000 dwellings newly constructed in the United Kingdom between 1970 and 1971, 168,000 were for the public sector and 196,000 for the private sector (*Social Trends*, 1972, p. 176). (Note that the housing stock changes by new construction, but also by conversions—a small net gain—and by losses due to slum clearance, fire, redevelopment, etc.)

The public sector construction is in response to statutory obligations and the stimulus of political pressures. The private sector construction is mostly by private developers (only a little is by households commissioning houses for themselves). The private developer supplies in response to the offer of money.

HOUSING MARKETS

Households desire dwellings, dwellings are provided. But how do people make their housing desires known? How do they get hold of the housing they want? How do the providers know what housing to provide? How do the providers contact the people who want the housing? The shorthand answer to all those questions is: housing demand and housing supply interact in the housing market. But what does that mean? How does the interaction take place? What is the housing market?

The first point is that it is not helpful to talk about one housing market, but about many housing markets which interact with each other. It is necessary thus to divide the housing market for two reasons. One is that the *supply* of housing is very varied. Unlike cars and most other commodities no two houses are identical: even seemingly identical dwellings vary in their locations. The other reason is that the *demand* for housing is varied. Different households want houses of different sizes, different types, different locations, etc. And a household may not be able to buy a house and wants to rent instead.

For example, when my family moved from London to Birmingham we were looking for a house to buy, of an older design, with four bedrooms, a short distance from my work, with a good garden, and facing the right direction so as to get the afternoon sun in the garden. So our housing market was specified by: tenure, design or style, size, location, orientation. Other people might not be so choosy, and might want to specify their housing market by: tenure, size, location only. (We omit price from the specification, not because it is unimportant, but because it is a dependent variable which is—for private housing if not for public housing—set in the market.)

So a fairly specific demand meets a fairly specific supply to create a fairly specific housing market. As a result there are many housing markets in one country. (For a detailed analysis of housing markets in one area see Kirwan and Ball, 1973.)

Nevertheless, housing markets interact with each other, with very important consequences. One reason for the interaction is that *demand* is to some extent substitutable between house types. For example, I might want to live and work in London. But if housing is too expensive, then I might look for a job in Birmingham and hence demand a house there. If I cannot get a house of the size or design that I want, I will, regretfully, look at other sizes and designs. And if I cannot afford to buy a house I might express my demand to rent a council house. The other reason for interactions between housing markets is that *supply* can be substituted between house types, to some extent. For example, I may own a house which I rent to tenants: but I get rid of those tenants and sell the house for owner-occupation. Or a local authority which found it uneconomic under the 1972 Housing Finance Act to build any more houses to rent, instead gave loans to local housing associations. The importance of interactions between housing markets can be seen from examples, such as the following.

Suppose there is oversupply in one sector of the private housing market. That might cause prices to drop (or not to rise so rapidly) in that sector. People in that sector who want to sell in order to move into another sector of the private housing market (e.g. a bigger house or another location) now have less money with which to buy. So demand in another sector is reduced.

The 1972 Housing Finance Act (now superseded) had the effect of increasing greatly council house rents for richer tenants. That caused many such tenants to try to buy instead. The increase in demand for private housing was probably one cause of the rapid increase in house prices which accompanied the introduction of the 1972 Act. One effect of that increase in house prices might have been to make house purchase impossible for poorer households. Instead, they tried to get a council house. So, as council housing lost its richer tenants, it gained more poorer tenants. Then the cost of rent rebate schemes increased.

It is useful now to look at some particular housing markets in a little more detail. What constitutes the market in which the demand for a particular type of house and the supply of that type interact? And how does the market work and respond to changes?

Private housing for sale

The market is the property advertisements in newspapers and the estate agents: in those ways are demanders and suppliers brought into contact with each other. Usually the supplier states a price. If the demand at that price is high, the house sells quickly. Other suppliers notice that (or are advised of it by estate agents) and the next time that kind of house is supplied, the asking price is set higher. Asking prices can fall as well as climb. If the supplier is completely uncertain what price to ask for (e.g. because the market has been changing very rapidly, or because very few houses of that type are offered for sale) the supplier may auction the house and in that way get the highest possible price. (That happened in Britain in 1972 when prices were rising so quickly that suppliers did not know where to set the price, and in particular did not want to set it too low.)

In that way, the suppliers and demanders come together and housing is exchanged. If supply and demand are unequal at a particular price, the price will change, which will alter both demand and supply so that they move towards equality.

Private housing for rent

The market is again advertisements in newspapers, also estate agents, and in addition notices in shop windows, accommodation agencies, lodgings officers. If supply and demand for a particular type of housing are unequal at a particular price, in the short run there may be queues or vacant dwellings (e.g. on Friday evenings in London there are queues for telephone kiosks by people wanting to rent property advertised in the Friday evening papers). In time, prices will change in response to an imbalance, and supply and demand will both move in the direction of equality (e.g. if there is excess demand, prices will rise, which will decrease demand—people share dwellings, take smaller dwellings, move out of the city—and increase supply—large houses are converted into small flats, purpose-designed blocks of flats are built, etc.).

There may, however, be laws to prevent rents responding freely to supply and demand conditions: usually such laws are to hold down rents (e.g. the registration of rents introduced by the 1965 Rent Act). If rents are held down in that way, demand will exceed supply. Then queues will form for available properties, or a black market will appear (e.g. demanding "key money" or premiums—both outlawed in the 1965 Rent Act).

Public housing for rent

Here the market is the Housing Manager's office. He has a list of available dwellings and a list of people who want dwellings. If the demand is greater than the supply, he usually has a points system by which he allocates the dwellings to the most needy, or the most deserving households.

If supply and demand are grossly imbalanced, he takes the problem to the Housing Committe of the Local Authority (or to the New Town Development Corporation). For example, there are 10,000 names on the housing list, new names are being entered at the rate of 1000 a year, and names are being taken off at the rate of only 200 a year. Or: I cannot let blocks of flats built before 1910 in remote locations.

It is the responsibility of the local authority to decide the allocation method and to decide what to do if supply and demand are grossly unequal. But in Britain the choices which a local authority can make are severely circumscribed by central government (e.g. the 1972 Housing Finance Act took most financial decisions out of the hands of the local council, the 1975 Housing Rents and Subsidies Act put some of them back, but retained the right to set rents). The market for housing association dwellings works in a similar way.

(Note that some of the ideas in this lecture are developed in more detail in Chapter 9.)

INDEX TO REFERENCES IN CHAPTER 5

BRADSHAW, J., 1972, "The concept of social need", *New Society*, 30th March 1972.

Census 1971, "Great Britain County Reports: general explanatory notes", HMSO, London.

CROFTON, B. and WEBSTER, D., 1974, "Improving housing allocation", *The Planner*, vol. 60, no. 8.

CULLINGWORTH, J. B., 1969, "Housing analysis", in Cullingworth, J. B. and Orr, S. C. (eds.), *Regional and Urban Studies*, Allen & Unwin, London.

Housing in the North West Region, 1970, North West Economic Planning Council, Manchester.

Housing Statistics Great Britain, 1969, no. 14, *Projections of Future Number of Potential Households*, HMSO, London.

KIRWAN, R. and BALL, M., 1973, "The micro-economic analysis of a local housing market", papers of the 1973 Urban Economics Conference, Centre for Environmental Studies, London.

Ministry of Housing and Local Government, *Report of the Committee on Housing in Greater London* (The Milner Holland Report), CMND 2605, HMSO, London.

SHANKLAND, COX & ASSOCIATES, 1968, *Ipswich Draft Basic Plan*, HMSO, London.

Social Trends, no. 6, 1975, HMSO, London.

WATSON, C. J. *et al.*, 1973, *Estimating Local Housing Needs*, CURS, The University of Birmingham.

FURTHER READING FOR CHAPTER 5

CULLINGWORTH, J. B., 1960, *Housing Needs and Planning Policy*, Routledge & Kegan Paul, London, part I.

CULLINGWORTH, J. B., 1969, "Housing analysis", in Cullingworth, J. B. and Orr, S. C. (eds.), *Regional and Urban Studies*, Allen & Unwin, London.

DONNISON, D. V., 1967, *The Government of Housing*, Penguin, Harmondsworth.

HARLOE, M. *et al.*, 1974, *The Organisation of Housing*, Heinemann, London.

HIRSCH, W. Z., 1973, *Urban Economic Analysis*, McGraw Hill, New York, chapter 3.

NEEDLEMAN, L., 1965, *The Economics of Housing*, Staples Press, London.

MURIE, A., NINER, P. and WATSON, C., 1976, *Housing Policy and the Housing System*, Allen & Unwin, London.

CHAPTER 6

People and Industry

INTRODUCTION

The city is the locus of a set of interactions which is crucial to our industrialised capitalist society—the interactions in which "wage labour" (as Marx called it) is exchanged for money. So important is this exchange that one of the most important functions of the city is as a labour market—i.e. as the location for the exchange.

People want work (whether because they enjoy it, or because they want the money it brings, is irrelevant here) so they *supply* their *labour*. Industry wants productive processes performing, some of which can be done only with the assistance of people. (Problems of industrial relations would disappear, and employers' lives become easier, if labour as a factor of production could be dispensed with. But with what would people then buy the commodities produced by industry?) So industry *demands labour* (probably as reluctantly as most people supply it).

PEOPLE SUPPLYING LABOUR

The economic unit within which most people live and for which most decisions on personal expenditure are made is the *household* (see Chapter 5). So it is the household which wants income to buy consumer goods and services. And most households with heads under retirement age rely on earnings from employment for their incomes. (There are other sources of household income—e.g. investments, welfare payments—but for most households those sources are secondary.)

So it is, accurately, households which supply labour. Each household (unless the head is retired) has to supply at least one income earner (the "primary" worker) and sometimes supplies more than one (the "secondary" workers—e.g. married women, older children living at home. In 1971 the average number of economically active persons per private household in England and Wales was 1.38: Census, 1971).

However, most data on labour supply are analysed by persons, not by households. So the labour which a given population supplies has to be studied by looking at the constituent individuals. The relationship between the individual members of the population and the labour supply is called the *activity rate* (or the participation rate). The activity rate of a given population (e.g. the population of England, or of Birmingham, or all married males aged over 60 and living in Worcestershire) is the number of workers supplied by a representative 100 members of the population. On what does activity rate depend? Why is it that 100 members of one population supply more labour than 100 members of another population?

Age

Apart from a little part-time work, people below the school-leaving age (16 from 1973) are not allowed to work. And after the minimum school-leaving age, many people remain in full-time education (and hence out of full-time work) for several years. At the other end of the life span, men qualify for old age pensions at 65 and women at 60. So above those ages, most people retire from the labour force. And approaching those ages, health worsens so an increasing proportion of people are unable to work.

Sex

In a family with children, it is usually the woman, not the man, who stays at home and looks after the children. So women of child-bearing age offer a smaller labour supply than do men of the same age.

Marital status

A man's marital status has little effect on his labour supply, but for a woman it is different. For example, if she is married she is likely to be kept out of the labour market by having to look after children. But if she is divorced she may have to go out to work, in spite of young children, because she is the only earner in the household.

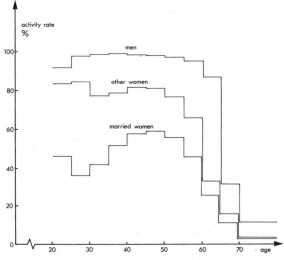

Fig. 6.1. Activity rates in Britain, 1971.

So age, sex, and marital status affect the labour which a given population supplies (see Fig. 6.1 from Census 1971 Summary Tables). But that is not all: other things too affect the labour supply. The labour supplied by one group of 100 people may be different from that supplied by another group of 100, although both groups are identical in age, sex and marital status. Why?

Employment opportunity

The primary workers need to work to provide household income; but the financial need for secondary workers to find jobs may not be pressing. For example, a married woman may take work if it is readily available, but not otherwise (see for example, Taylor, 1968). (By physical planning, work can be made convenient for married women—e.g. by planning small pockets of industrial land inside housing estates, see Shankland, Cox & Associates, 1968, p. 131. If the work were inconveniently located, fewer married women would take it.)

Income opportunity

A related factor is the amount of money to be earned from jobs: but empirical evidence about the effect of this is scarce. If wages are high, does that tempt more secondary workers into the labour market? Or does it enable the household to be more easily satisfied with the income from the primary worker, in which case the labour supply from secondary workers would diminish?

Tradition and convention

Some examples will make the point here. During the first World War, the tradition was broken that women did not drive buses. When my parents married, my mother automatically gave up her work, interesting and useful though it was: that was the convention in middle-class households at that time. Now, an increasing proportion of married women work, and married women form an increasing proportion of the working population (*Social Trends*, no. 5, 1974).

Health is the last factor we shall mention: people in bad health cannot supply their labour. Activity rates in an area of poor health (e.g. mining valleys) are lower than in other areas for that reason. The above factors affect the labour *offered* onto the labour market by people. But not all the offers to do jobs may be taken up by industry. When that happens there is *unemployment*. (It is important to remember that activity rates are for people wanting to work, not just for those actually working: the rates calculated from the Census of Population are for persons "economically active" which means people in the labour market. But unemployment reduces the activity rates of secondary workers by affecting their perception of employment opportunities.)

Should unemployed people be counted as part of the labour supply? In order to answer that, we have to distinguish between four types of unemployment—frictional, incapacitated persons, structural, and insufficient aggregate demand. *Frictional* unemployment occurs while people change their jobs: they are out of work temporarily. Such unemployment is unavoidable, and is necessary for industrial and personal change. Some *incapacitated persons* are unable to work because of physical or mental illness: still they register as unemployed, out of hope or in order to draw welfare payments. Such unemployment is unavoidable. Avoidable unemployment occurs when there are people who want to work and who are fully capable of working, but who nevertheless do not work because there are not enough jobs available of the type they can do. The number of jobs may be inadequate because of *structural* changes in the economy (e.g. a change from coal to oil causing unemployment among miners) or because the demand for industrial output in general is too low (*aggregate demand deficiency*), as in a general slump.

Now we can answer the question: Should unemployed people be counted as part of the labour supply? with the answer: yes, if their unemployment is avoidable; no, if it is unavoidable. So how much unemployment is unavoidable? It is very rare for unemployment in any area to fall below 1% of all insured workers, even in times of economic boom and great labour scarcity. So we can say, roughly, that 1% of all labour supplied will be unavoidably unemployed and hence not part of the effective labour supply.

So far we have discussed the labour supply in terms of number of workers only. There is, of course, another important property of the labour supply—the *occupational skills* offered. The ability to perform a particular job depends upon aptitude, experience, and training: so a person can offer some occupational skills and not others. People can learn new skills, but that takes time. So at any one time, a given population will be able to offer a given set of occupational skills, the set depending on the previous experiences of the members of the population.

Let us tie together this section by considering the labour supplied by a given population—say all those living in Birmingham CB in 1966. What are the important properties of that labour supply, important (that is) to industry which might demand it? First, its size, 551,470 persons (this information is taken from the sample Census 1966, Economic Activity County Leaflet, Warwickshire). Second, its occupational composition: 2270 farmers, 131,920 engineering workers, 74,330 clerical workers, etc. One other property which might be important to industry (although possibly decreasingly so—see below) is its composition by sex: of the 131,920 engineering workers 102,150 were male and 29,770 female, of the 74,330 clerical workers 19,670 were male and 54,660 female, etc. What is it that caused the residents of Birmingham in 1966 to supply labour with those properties? It was the number, age, sex, marital status, and health of the residents, it was the residents' previous experiences, skills and abilities, it was the opportunities offered the residents by the available industry (supply is not independent of demand), and it was the traditions and conventions surrounding work in the Midlands.

INDUSTRY DEMANDING LABOUR

We shall start at the beginning, by explaining how we shall use the word "industry", for much confusion can be caused by obscurity here. In everyday use, industry means factories. In statutory town and country planning, industrial land uses are carefully specified and industry has a meaning similar to its everyday meaning. In economics, industry is the formal production of goods and services. It is in its economic sense that we shall use the word. So industry includes the production of food, timber, slate, etc. (extractive industries) and insurance, repairs, TV programmes, etc. (service industries) as well are cars, pens, clothes, etc. (manufacturing industries, usually in factories). And it includes formal production (i.e. where the producers are paid for their work) but not informal production (so my growing vegetables in my garden is not part of industry).

If there is a given amount of industry, specified by the nature and value of its output, what are the main things it will look for when it demands labour?

Occupation

There are certain jobs which firms want doing, and those jobs are specified by occupation. So, for example, a firm might want 20 copy typists, 10 van drivers, a storekeeper, 4 men to maintain the vans, and a tea lady.

(Note that it is very important to be clear about the distinction between the occupational structure and the industrial structure of the labour force. Industry is classified by the nature of the output—e.g. the steel industry, the coal industry. Labour is classified by occupation, by the jobs people do—e.g. typist, bookeeper. Any industry will usually employ more than one occupation: any occupation will usually work in more than one industry—e.g. a typist in a car firm or in a university. The confusion arises because a labour force can be classified both by what the workers do—the occupational structure—and by the output of the firms for which the people work—the industrial structure. A particular source of confusion is the term "service workers": are they people who work in service industries, or people with service occupations, such as managers?)

Sex

The demand by industry for a certain occupation may automatically be a demand for a certain gender of worker, because some jobs can be done only by men (e.g. mining coal) or by women (e.g. wet nursing). Apart from that, industry may demand a certain sex composition of the labour force, either for financial reasons (until the Equal Pay Act 1970 comes into full force, it is possible to pay women less than men for doing the same job) or for convention (e.g. it is expected that the managing director will be a man, the office cleaner a woman: there is now a law that prevents sex discrimination in employment).

So industry demands labour and the demand is specified by occupation and by sex. What affects the size of that demand?

Industrial output

To industry, labour is a factor of production, necessary for producing the final output, be it repaired cars, television programmes, or cured children. The relationship between the number of workers and the final output can then be described in a standardised way as the output per worker. So, if output increases, so will labour demand.

However, labour demand might not increase in the same proportion as output increases. At larger outputs, production may be more efficient, so output per worker may be greater when 100 workers are employed than when 10 workers are employed. Also, the occupational composition of the additional labour demand may be different from the average occupational composition: if 1000 units are produced per week using 10 lathe operators and 2 office workers per unit of output, in order to produce an additional 100 units per week may require only 11 extra workers per unit of output, 10 of them lathe operators and 1 office worker.

Substitutability of labour

To industry, labour is just one factor of production among several. So if the job which a man does could be done by another factor of production (usually a machine), industry can consider changing its production methods (e.g. substituting capital for labour). If that is done, output per worker increases: so, for a given output, industry demands less labour. Moreover, substitution usually changes the skills required (e.g. instead of being strong enough to use a shovel you need to be skilled enough to use an excavator). Then, for a given output, the occupational composition of the labour which industry wants will be different.

An example might make this section clearer. In the year 1972–3 the Central Electricity Generating Board sold 203,539 million kWh of electricity, most of which it also produced. That was 7.9% more than in the previous year. However, the number of employees, far from increasing, fell by 2.5%: sales per employee rose by 10.7%. How was that achieved? Partly by better organisation, partly by substituting capital for labour: the capital employed rose by 2.0% and the capital per employee by 4.6% (CEGB, 1973).

THE LOCATIONS OF LABOUR SUPPLY AND LABOUR DEMAND

The household supplies labour, so the labour supply is located at the household's *residence*. Industry demands labour, so the labour demand is located at the industry's *establishment*—the factory, the shop, the farm, the hospital. The physical link between the locations of labour supply and demand is made by the *journey-to-work*—the worker leaves his or her home and travels to the establishment.

A residential suburb contains many more people wanting to work than there are jobs available in the suburb. So, even if all the jobs in the suburb were filled by local residents, there would still be an outflow of workers to jobs elsewhere. It is likely of course, that many of the local jobs are taken by non-local workers, travelling into the area: in that case, the outflow of workers is greater. In both cases there is a net outflow of labour: a residential suburb is a *net exporter* of labour. Conversely, a city centre, an industrial estate, a market town in a rural region are all usually *net importers* of labour: they receive net inflows of workers.

An area which is neither a net importer nor a net exporter of labour is said to have a *job ratio* of 100: a net importer has a job ratio greater than 100, a net exporter a job ratio less than 100.

TABLE 6.1. LABOUR SUPPLY, LABOUR USED, AND JOURNEYS-TO-WORK, BIRM-INGHAM C.B. 1966

Labour supply		Labour used	
residents in employment	538,820	total working population	646,470
Area of workplace		Area of residence	
Birmingham CB	495,630	Birmingham CB	495,630
elsewhere	43,190	elsewhere	150,840
West Bromwich CB	5,160	Solihull CB	25,690
Solihull CB	8,700	Sutton Coldfield MB	19,520
etc.		etc.	

Source: Sample Census 1966, Workplace and Transport Tables, Part I, tables 2 and 3.
Note: The "residents in employment" excludes those who are economically active but out of employment.
The table shows that Birmingham CB is a net importer of labour. The job ratio it 646,470/538,820 = 1.2 = 120.

Examples of the above can be taken from the Census of Population, which records labour supply (residents economically active) by location of residence, and labour used (not strictly labour demand) by location of work place, both for local authority areas. Also, the Census records journeys-to-work, so the links between the locations of supply and of demand are recorded. (Birmingham is used as an example in Table 6.1.)

LABOUR MARKETS

Labour supply and labour demand interact, and the results are people working, jobs being done. For analysing that interaction we are interested in two properties of the jobs done—the nature of the job (or the occupation of the worker), and the location of the workplace. So there is not just one labour market, but many labour markets, each specified by the occupation and by the location of the workplace. Some examples are—the labour market for typists in central Birmingham, the labour market for skilled car workers in Coventry, the labour market for neurosurgeons in the United States.

Over how big an area does a labour market extend? In the short term, the only people who consider applying for a job are those (with the appropriate skills) who live within a reasonable journey-to-work distance of the workplace. So the journey-to-work possibilities and what is considered to be a reasonable work journey set the limits of the labour market. In the longer term, people living outside those limits may consider moving house in order to take a job. Whether or not a person does move for a job depends on ambition and on the number of openings for that person's occupation: a typist in Birmingham need never look outside Birmingham for a job, whereas a neurosurgeon in Birmingham may find his job becoming unsatisfactory, at a time when the only other openings available for neurosurgeons are in Glasgow or Manchester, and if he is especially ambitious he might even consider draining to the United States along with other medical brains. So, in the longer term, the extent of the labour market varies with occupation: the market for typists working in central Birmingham might extend 10 miles around Birmingham, whereas the labour market for neurosurgeons working in New York might extend as far as Birmingham and even India. (In the longer term still, jobs might move to the workers, rather than workers to the jobs—see later.)

For some purposes it is useful to consider the *local labour market*. That is "an area in which there is concentration of employment within which most resident workers can change jobs without changing their place of residence. Its main feature is that the bulk of the area's working population habitually seeks employment within the area and that local employers recruit most of their labour from its constituent communities" (Hunter, 1969, p. 54). It is, therefore, a geographical area which contains most of the occupational labour markets which centre upon a concentration of employment. (For an example of an analysis of, and planning for, a local labour market see Shankland, Cox & Associates, 1968, append. E. And for an example of an analysis of an unbalanced labour market see IAS/LA/4, 1975.)

How do the buyers and sellers of labour contact each other? That question can be rephrased: How does industry make known its demands for labour to those who supply labour? because the reverse process—people offering their labour publicly—is much less common, and is done mainly by people who are unemployed.

The way the contact is made depends on the characteristics of the labour market. If it is small in area, firms advertise in the local papers and notify vacancies to the employment exchanges. If the market is wider, firms advertise in the national papers. And if the job is a specialist occupation which has its own journals, advertisements are placed in those journals too (e.g. vacancies for social workers advertised in *New Society*).

Let us now consider how labour supply and demand interact *within one labour market*. We shall do that by taking one case—e.g. the labour market for typists to work in central Birmingham, a market which may extend (say) 10 miles from the centre of Birmingham.

Firms in central Birmingham which want typists advertise vacancies and offer a wage for the job: workers living within the labour market and wanting such work see the advertisements and apply. Firms engage and employ typists. Insofar as one typing job is like another, all firms are able to get the same sort of worker by offering the same wage.

Suppose that, at the wage offered, many more typists apply than there are jobs. The firms may lower wages (or, more likely, not raise them to keep pace with increases in other wages). At that lower wage, firms are willing to employ more typists, and fewer typists apply for the jobs. If the wage is set by trade union negotiation or by a Wages Council, firms are not able to reduce an oversupply in that way: instead, they become very choosey about whom they employ.

If, at the wage offered, firms cannot get enough typists, they try to increase supply by making the jobs more attractive—e.g. by offering more money or by offering better fringe benefits. More people then apply. From where do those extra people come?—from people previously not working (e.g. housewives), from people previously doing other types of work (e.g. people with typing skills working in shops), from typists living outside the labour market area. (In the latter two cases, the labour market is interacting with other labour markets—see later.) If firms are not allowed to raise wages (e.g. because of a prices and incomes law), or if they are unsuccessful in attracting more labour, they try to reduce their labour demands by substituting capital for labour.

How does interaction *between labour markets* take place? If firms employing typists in central Birmingham reduce their demands and employ fewer workers, the now-unemployed typists may look to other areas for jobs—e.g. to Wolverhampton, when they increase the extent of the labour market, and hence the labour supply, for typing jobs in Wolverhampton. If the firms in central Birmingham want to employ more typists, those firms may try to extend their labour market by cutting into other market areas. Or suppose that the supply of typists living within 10 miles of Birmingham city centre changes (e.g. by vocational training in schools, or by emigration into greener housing areas): then the supply of typists in other labour markets changes. In such ways there can be interaction between different geographical labour markets for the same occupation.

The effect of a reduction in demand by city centre firms for typists may be different: people who were previously typists get jobs in shops instead. If the demand for typists increases, shopworkers attend evening classes in order to learn how to type. In such ways there can be interaction between different occupational labour markets in the same geographical area. In the short term, however, interactions between geographical labour markets are usually more important than between occupational labour markets, because it is easier for most workers to change their work journeys than their skills.

If the labour demands for all occupations within the same wide geographical area (the local labour market) change in the same direction (e.g. a decline in demand for all skills in the West Midlands conurbation), then neither changes in work journeys nor in skills will be able to rectify the resulting imbalance between supply and demand. So, if, for example, demand is greater than supply over a large area and there is excess supply in other areas, people migrate from one local labour market to the other (as happened, for example, in the famous "drift to the South" from Scotland and the north of England in the 1950's). In such ways, widely separated geographical labour markets can interact with each other.

Finally, the importance of government intervention in labour markets must be recognised. Some of the effects of government on labour markets are caused by actions undertaken for other reasons—e.g. incomes legislation designed to reduce inflation, the factory inspectors whose job is to reduce industrial accidents. But also the government intervenes directly and deliberately in the workings of labour markets, for two main reasons. One is to make the labour market work more smoothly: for example, one of the purposes of official Employment Exchanges is to bring together buyers and sellers of labour, to the advantage of both. The other reason for deliberate government intervention in the labour market is to rectify long-term imbalances in supply and demand. If there is, in a particular occupational market, an imbalance which is not becoming less serious quickly enough by the "natural" market forces of people changing jobs or moving, then the government may introduce training and retraining schemes (e.g. the retraining schemes for redundant coal miners). If there is, in all occupational labour markets in one area, a persistent imbalance between supply and demand, the government may try to change the total supply of, or demand for, jobs in that area. So, in the boom conditions of the 1960's, the government tried to stop firms expanding in Birmingham and tried to move Birmingham firms to other areas. And in the North East which suffers from chronic unemployment, the government has been trying since the 1930's to persuade new firms to locate there.

INDEX TO REFERENCES IN CHAPTER 6

CEGB, 1973, *Annual Report, 1972/73*, vol. 2, Central Electricity Generating Board, London.

Census 1971, Economic Activity, part I, HMSO, London.

Census 1971, Summary Tables, 1% Sample, HMSO, London.

HUNTER, L. C., 1969, "Planning and the labour market", in Cullingworth, J. B. and Orr, S. C. (eds.), *Regional and Urban Studies*, Allen & Unwin, London.

IAS/LA/4, 1975, *Labour Market Study*, Department of the Environment, London.

Sample Census 1966, England and Wales, *Economic Activity County Leaflets, Warwickshire*, HMSO, London.

Sample Census 1966, England and Wales, *Workplace and Transport Tables*, part I, HMSO, London.

SHANKLAND, COX & ASSOCIATES, 1968, *Ipswich Draft Basic Plan*, HMSO, London.

Social Trends, no. 5, 1974, HMSO, London.

TAYLOR, J., 1968, "Hidden female labour reserves", *Regional Studies*, vol. 2, no. 2.

FURTHER READING FOR CHAPTER 6

BROWN, E. H. P., 1962, *The Economics of Labour*, Yale University Press.

HIRSCH, W. Z., 1973, *Urban Economic Analysis*, McGraw Hill, New York, Chapter 5.

HUNTER, L. C., 1969, "Planning and the labour market", in Cullingworth, J. B. and Orr, S. C. (eds.), *Regional and Urban Studies*, Allen & Unwin, London.

PATERSON, J. H., 1972, *Land Work, and Resources*, Arnold, London, especially chapter 2.

CHAPTER 7

People and Commercial Services

SERVICES COMMERCIALLY PROVIDED

In this chapter we try to explain how certain services are demanded
and how they are supplied. We are concerned with services which
are provided commercially and privately for a profit, which are used
directly by the final consumer (i.e. by private households), and which
cannot be transported (as a result of which buyers have to travel
to where the services are produced). Examples of such services are—
retailing services provided by shops which sell goods (e.g. grocers,
shoe shops), personal services provided by shops which sell services
(e.g. hairdressers, betting shops, travel agents), personal services provided by offices (e.g. family solicitors, estate agents), entertainment
services (e.g. cinemas, night clubs, pubs, cafes). The services with
which we are not concerned are those which are publicly provided
(e.g. education, justice, welfare), those which are charitably provided
(e.g. religion), those which are inputs to industry (e.g. warehousing,
industrial accountants), and those which can be transported (e.g. TV
shows, mail order shopping, life assurance)

We shall describe and classify the commercial services which
are our concern as—retailing services, professional services,
and entertainment services. And we shall see later that the property of these services that causes us most problems is that they
cannot be transported, so the demander has to travel to the
supplier.

THE DEMAND FOR, AND THE SUPPLY OF, SERVICES

Demand

The services we are considering are very varied, and the demands for the services are similarly varied. Let us consider *retailing services* first.

When people buy goods, they want—a shop which sells those goods, preferably several shops selling the same or similar goods so that the shopper can compare and choose, cheap prices and good service, public transport or car parking, a pleasant environment, and not to travel very far (unless the shopping trip is combined with another trip such as a journey to work or a family outing). When people want to buy services from service shops (e.g. a haircut) the things they demand are similar.

(The value of the effective money demand for retailing services can be estimated as follows. Expenditure in retail shops selling goods in 1966 in Britain was £213 per person (Board of Trade, 1970). Average gross profit margin in retail shops is around 30%. So expenditure per person per year on the retailing services provided by shops selling goods was around £64 in 1966. Note that this is expressed in terms of individuals, although the real unit of consumption is the household.)

The demand for *professional services*—e.g. for the personal services of an accountant or solicitor—is irregular, unlike the demand to buy food or toothpaste. Also, the demander is more likely to have a particular supplier in mind—Mr. X has been recommended as a very clever and discreet solicitor. That means that the demand by the buyer of the professional service for an easy journey and to be able to compare suppliers is less than when he goes shopping. Nevertheless, the buyer does not want an inconvenient journey, and some buyers choose a professional firm at random and therefore want to know where the "professional quarter" is.

The demand that the service be conveniently located and easily accessible applies to some *entertainment services* (e.g. a visit to the cinema) and not to others (e.g. a dinner-dance). For with some entertainments the journey might be positively enjoyable, part of the fun, not just a chore as is the journey to shops. Hence operas at Glynde-bourne, dinners in old castles, the evenings at the nice pub in the country (see Clawson and Knetsch, 1971, who include the journey to and from the recreational destination as part of the recreational experience).

Another way in which the demand for recreational services is dif-ferent from the demand for retailing or professional services is that it is often not a very specific demand. If you want to buy cheese, a baker's shop is no use to you, and if you want the services of a solicitor, an accountant's office is of no help. But if you want a "night out" you can go for a meal, or to the cinema, or if all those fail you can buy some beer and sit in front of the TV all night. Demand is substitutable between different types of entertain-ment services.

Supply

The supply of services can be studied in two parts—the supply of the services which the consumers want (e.g. selling food, con-veyancing of property, providing a concert), and the supply of the buildings in which the services are provided (e.g. the property deve-loper building new shops and offices). It is possible to divide the study into those two parts for several reasons, the more important of which are as follows. Usually, the building is supplied by a person or firm different from the person or firm which supplies the services from that building (e.g. the shopkeeper usually rents his shop). The buildings from which services are supplied are often very flexible and can accommodate a wide range of service-providing activities (e.g. the same building can be used as a betting shop, a shoe shop, an estate agent's, a cafe. And although cinemas are rather inflexible, they have been used as theatres and as bowling alleys). For many commercial services, the cost of converting a building for special use is small: so the providers of services can move easily and quickly into and out of commercial buildings. In contrast, the supply of new buildings takes a long time, and the completed buildings last for many years.

The supply of the actual *services* is by private persons or firms, in response to a money demand, and is motivated by a desire to make money and earn a livelihood. The supply of the *buildings* is mostly from existing stock: the annual additions to the stock by new buildings are a small proportion of total supply. The demand is a money demand from the suppliers of services (the shopkeepers, the hairdressers, etc.), a demand either to buy or to rent. The supply, of new and existing buildings, is private and motivated by money. (In economic terms, the demand for such buildings is a "derived demand", derived from the demand by private households for commercial services.)

Interactions between supply and demand

The demand for *retailing and professional services* is fairly specific (e.g. a household wants to buy food) and is backed by money, by a willingness to pay for the services. The supply of those services is in direct response to that demand. If demand increases, supply will increase, and vice versa. The response of supply to demand will be considered in two parts, as before.

The supply of *services* can respond very rapidly to changes in demand because, as we noted above, existing buildings can be quickly and cheaply adapted for the supply of a wide range of services. So a grocer's shop takes over from the chemist, storage space above a shop becomes a small estate agent's, a young hairdresser gets permission to convert the ground floor of his house into a salon.

The supply of the *buildings* from which the services are provided is much more sluggish, and can respond only very slowly to changes in demand. So we often find such buildings in places where there seems to be insufficient demand for them. For example, we find many small shops still trading in the inner areas of cities although most of the previous residents have moved away. In contrast, we find new housing estates, even whole new towns, with too few shops and a narrow range of service facilities. And we notice applications to build hypermarkets or to redevelop town centre shopping areas in anticipation of demand, an expectation which may or may not be fulfilled.

The demand for *entertainment services* is not very specific, as we noted earlier. For that reason, it is only partly true to say that supply responds to demand: also, demand responds to supply. If an entrepreneur starts a night club in a previously sedate small town, that supply may well stimulate a demand for nightclub entertainment.

The question of location

So far, we have ignored the question of location, although both the supply of, and the demand for, commercial services are located in space. Demand comes from housholds, so is located where the people live. Supply is located in service buildings.

As, for most services, supply is in response to demand, the suppliers choose a location by reference to the location of demand, to where the customers live. Hence we can treat the location of demand as given, and the location of supply as variable. Moreover, as (again for most services) the demand is to travel not very far to buy the service, the suppliers want to locate near the demanders. Finally, as most supply is from existing buildings and can move quickly and easily into and out of those buildings, suppliers can change their locations quite quickly in response to changes in the location of demand.

So we have to ask the following *locational questions* about the interaction of supply and demand. With demand in a given location, how do the suppliers of services and of service buildings decide where to locate? When the supply has been thus located, how do the demanders decide to which locations of supply to travel? There are several location theories which try to answer one or both of those questions.

LOCATION THEORIES

Central place theory

This theory attempts to answer the two questions—how do suppliers choose a location? how do demanders choose a supply location?—by using the two key concepts of the demand threshold and the range of a service.

The *demand threshold* "is defined in terms of the minimum level required to support a service and can be expressed in terms of population and/or income. The threshold occurs when sales are just sufficient for the firm supplying the service to earn normal profits" (Richardson, 1969, p. 157). For example, a public house needs 250 people to support it, a bank 1,700 people (Paterson, 1972, Chap. 9). The *range* is the distance over which the service is supplied: there

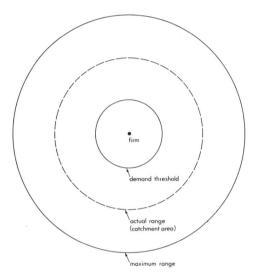

Fig. 7.1. The threshold and range of a service supplied by a firm.

is a maximum range for any service beyond which people will not travel to buy it. Those two concepts may be illustrated as in Fig. 7.1.

Using the two concepts it can be deduced that there will be an hierarchical spatial structure of service centres —i.e. discrete classes of service centres, classes which do not merge into each other, where the location of service centres relative to each other can be explained in terms of the location of population and transport routes (see Fig. 3.2). Richardson (1969, pp. 161–2) explains it as follows: "Assume an area supplied with *n* types of central goods, ranked in ascending order from 1 to n. Then the central place which supplies n (let us call it A) needs the largest market area. As many A centres will exist as there are threshold sales levels to support firms supplying good n. . . . All other central goods and services ($n–1$, $n–2$, . . . , 1) will also be supplied by A centres, and excess profits are possible in the supply of these. However, there will be some good, let us call it $n–i$, where purchasing power located in the interstices between the threshold market areas of A centres supplying good $n–i$ will justify further threshold market areas in these gaps. It will be more efficient for these gaps to be plugged by a second set of centres, which may be named B centres, supplying the good." And so on, with the possibility of C centres plugging the gaps between B centres, then D centres, etc. In that way, it may be deduced that there will be a central place hierarchy as demonstrated in Table 7.1.

That general theory is usually applied to a set of unrealistic geographical conditions (e.g. uniform distribution of population, a flat featureless plain) when it can be deduced that there will be a regular spacing of central places and that catchment areas will be in the form of nesting hexagonals (see, for example, Garner, 1967, p. 307). But we do not need those initial conditions. The general theory enables us to answer the two questions—How do suppliers decide where to locate? (i.e. where are the service centres?)—and How do

TABLE 7.1. HOW n TYPES OF GOOD ARE SUPPLIED BY M TYPES OF CENTRE

Centres	$n, n-1, \ldots$	Goods $n-i, n-$ $(i+1), \ldots$	$n-j, n-$ $(j+1), \ldots$	$\ldots$	$k, k-1, \ldots 1$
A	×	×	×	×	×
B		×	×	×	×
C			×	×	×
⋮				×	⋮
M					×

Source: after Richardson, 1969, p. 162.

demanders decide which supplier to visit? (i.e. where are the catchment areas around the service centres?)—with any set of initial geographical conditions. The only problem is that the more realistic the initial conditions, the more difficult it is to deduce the answers from the theory.

Spatial interaction theories

These theories attempt to answer the second question only, *viz.* with given locations of service suppliers, how do demanders choose

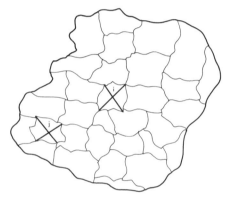

Fig. 7.2. A self-contained service area divided into *n* zones.

which supply location to use? Two types of explanation are used, the gravity approach and the intervening opportunities approach. Here we describe the more common one—the gravity approach—only.

Such theories start by taking an area which is self-contained in its service trade and dividing that area into *n* zones, of which two may be called *i* and *j* (see Fig. 7.2). The theories then state that a shopper in zone *i* is attracted to *all* shopping centres in the service area (e.g. the centre in zone *j*). The amount of money which the shopper spends in a shopping centre depends on two things—the attractiveness of the shopping centre (*A*), and the distance between the shopper and the centre (*d*). Therefore, over a given period of time (a year, say) the expenditure by all residents in one zone (*i*) in the shopping centre in another zone (*j*) is:

$$S_{ij} = K_i E_i A_j F(d_{ij})$$

where K_i = a constant, E_i = expenditure per year available in zone *i* for all shopping. Because the area is self-contained for service trade, the expenditure by zone *i* in all shopping centres in the area $\left(\sum_j S_{ij} \right)$ must be equal to the total shopping expenditure available in zone *i* (E_i). From that it can be calculated that:

$$K_i = \frac{1}{\sum\limits_j^n A_j F(d_{ij})}.$$

Therefore:

$$S_{ij} = \frac{E_i A_j F(d_{ij})}{\sum\limits_j^n A_j F(d_{ij})}.$$

Several versions of this theory have been developed, and are described and criticised in Distributive Trades EDC (1970, Chap. 3). For our present purpose all that we need to know is that they all give usable answers to the question: How do demanders decide which supplier to visit?

(There is another set of theories—rent theories—which try to answer the question: How do suppliers choose where to locate? We shall not describe them here because they are not yet operational. For a description see Distributive Trades EDC, 1970, Chap. 4.)

In Chapter 3 we described how central place theory could be used to explain the interactions between a town and its rural hinterland, how people visit the town from outside in order to buy services. And it is for explanations at those regional and sub-regional scales that central place theory was developed. (For an example of its application to sub-regional planning see "Deeside Planning Study" 1970, appendix D.) Are we right, then, to describe it as a location theory which can explain interactions *within* towns?

That question can be rephrased: Is central place theory applicable when distances between service centres are small and when the transport system enables people to be very mobile? Those conditions apply to some people and for some services in the South East Region, and central place theory has been tested there and found wanting (Schiller, 1971). The conditions of close service centres, good accessibility, and high mobility are present to an even greater degree within towns. So is it incorrect to apply central place theory there? (as was done, for example, in order to plan service centres within Ipswich—see Shankland, Cox & Associates, 1966, appendix E).

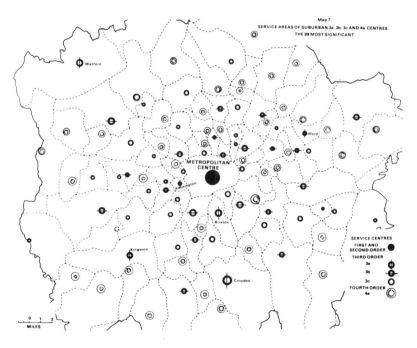

Fig. 7.3. Service centres in Greater London (from Carruthers, 1972, Service centres in Greater London, *Town Planning Review*, Vol. 33, by courtesy of the Liverpool University Press).

It is certainly very difficult to find catchment areas around the various service centres within a town. "The fact is", says the City of Birmingham Structure Plan (1973, p. 21), "that people living in the City have a wide choice of shopping centres and, therefore, tend to 'shop around' for goods and services and are not dependent on any one centre." So it is that surveys reveal not the catchment areas of central place theory but areas of variable influence, trade falling off with distance (Ambrose, 1968).

Such findings are inconsistent with central place theory, but are consistent with the spatial interaction theories. Do we say, therefore, that for application within towns spatial interaction theories should be used (as is already done quite widely—see, for example, Rhodes and Whitaker, 1967), and that central place theory should be reserved for application between towns?

No, we cannot say that. For spatial interaction theories predict differences in *size* between service centres but not differences in *function*. Yet we find both within towns: we find not only that some centres are bigger than others but also that the bigger centres contain a wider range of services. (See Fig. 7.3. Note: the service areas on this figure are predicted, not observed.) Only central place theory can explain differences in function as well as differences in size. Perhaps what is needed is a theory to apply within towns which combines both central place theory and spatial interaction theory (just as an attempt was made to combine those two theories for application between towns in *Regional Shopping Centres in North West England*, 1964).

MARKETS FOR SERVICES

The interaction between the demand for and the supply of a particular service creates, in such ways, a set of *geographical market areas* for that service. And we have seen that between towns the geographical market areas may be the catchment areas predicted by central place theory (where all the people within the catchment area of one centre travel to that centre, but immediately over the boundary of the catchment area all the people travel to another centre), and within towns there are more likely to be areas of influence (as you move away from one centre the attractive influence of that centre declines and of another centre increases).

Interactions between markets

Because the demand for most services if fairly specific, there is little interaction between the markets for different services. So if the market for accountancy services based in the centre of Birmingham changes, that is unlikely to have much effect on the market for estate agency services. The exceptions to that statement are the markets for entertainment services, because there is (as we have seen) much substitution between the demands for particular entertainments. So, if the market for one service changes (e.g. people spend more time and money "eating out" in the evenings), the markets for other entertainments are likely to change (e.g. people spend less time and money in cinemas). Moreover, because journeys to the source of the entertainment are often not regarded as a chore, the locational consequences of such interactions are hard to predict.

In contrast to the slight interaction between the markets for different services, there is much interaction between different geographical markets for the same service. Indeed, the aim of most shopkeepers and shopping developers is to cut into someone else's catchment area, to take away someone else's trade in that service. (Although, of course, if all competing suppliers tried to achieve that aim the result would be a massive surplus of shops.)

So it is very important to be able to predict the effects of changes in the supply of a service on the geographical markets for that service. How can such predictions be made? By using the location theories described above. For example, in the short-term the question is: with a given change in supply, how will the demanders change the suppliers which they visit (i.e. how will market areas change)? Both central place theory and spatial interaction theory can be used to answer that question. In the longer term, another question arises: with the changed market areas, how will suppliers change their locations? Only central place theory can answer that question.

An important example was the proposal to build a new regional shopping centre on a virgin site at Haydock Park at the junction of the M6 and the East Lancashire Road, half-way between Manchester and Liverpool. If that were built, what trade would it capture and from what existing centres would the catches be made? Then, with many existing centres taking much less trade, would they lose their shops and offices? Would that leave the way open for more new service centres to operate? An ambitious attempt to answer those questions was made by *Regional Shopping Centres in North West England* (1964).

Such predictions, although usually on a smaller scale, are the "bread-and-butter" work of shopping consultants. For example, when the local paper announces "£1,500,000 would be town's annual trade loss to hypermarket" (*Sutton Coldfield News*, 7th July 1972), it is reporting the prediction made at a planning appeal by the shopping consultant for the developer of the hypermarket. (And in that case, the prediction was influential in having the appeal rejected: the planning inspector did not think it desirable that the surrounding towns should lose that much trade.)

INDEX TO REFERENCES IN CHAPTER 7

AMBROSE, P. J., 1968, "Intra-urban shopping patterns", *Town Planning Review*, vol. 38.

Board of Trade, 1970, *Report of the Census of Distribution and Other Services*, 1966, HMSO, London.

City of Birmingham Structure Plan, 1973, *Report of Survey: Shopping*, Birmingham.

CLAWSON, M. and KNETSCH, J., 1971, *The Economics of Outdoor Recreation*, John Hopkins Press. Baltimore.

Deeside Planning Study, 1970, Shankland, Cox & Associates, London.

Distributive Trades EDC, 1970, *Urban Models in Shopping Studies*, National Economic Development Office, London.

GARNER, B. J., 1967, "Models of urban geography and settlement location", in Chorley, R. J. and Haggett, P. (eds.), *Socio-economic Models in Geography*, Methuen, London.

PATERSON, J. H., 1972, *Land, Work, and Resources*, Arnold, London.

Regional Shopping Centres in North West England, 1964, Manchester University Dept. of Town Planning, Manchester.

RHODES, T. and WHITAKER, R., 1967, "Forecasting shopping demand", *Journal of the Town Planning Institute*, vol. 53, no. 5.

RICHARDSON, H. W., 1969, *Regional Economics*, Weidenfeld & Nicholson, London.

SCHILLER, R. K., 1971, "Location trends of specialist services", *Regional Studies*, vol. 5, no. 1.

SHANKLAND, COX & ASSOCIATES, 1966, *Expansion of Ipswich*, HMSO, London.

FURTHER READING FOR CHAPTER 7

BURTON, T. L. and NOAD, P. A., 1968, *Recreation Research Methods*, Occasional paper no. 3, Centre for Urban and Regional Studies, University of Birmingham.

DANIELS, P. W., 1975, *Office Location*, Bell, London.

Distributive Trades EDC, 1970, *Urban Models in Shopping Studies*, National Economic Development Office, London.

KRUEKEBERG, D. A. and SILVER, A. L., 1974, *Urban Planning Analysis*, John Wiley, New York, chapter 9.

MARRIOTT, O., 1969, *The Property Boom*, Pan Books, London.

PATERSON, J. H., 1972, *Land, Work, and Resources*, Arnold, London, chapter 9.

See also further reading recommended for Chapter 3.

CHAPTER 8

Interactions between Activities and Locations

ACTIVITY SYSTEMS

In Chapters 3, 4, 5, 6 and 7, we talked about activities interacting between a town and its region and about activities interacting with buildings. In so doing we had to describe the *locations* of the activities. But little was said about how those interactions affect the location of the activities *within the town*. In this chapter we shall describe how the interactions of activities, people, and buildings cause activities to cluster into *functional areas*, and how functional areas interact with each other.

Chapin (1965, p. 224) has used the term "activity systems" to describe "behaviour patterns of individuals, families, institutions, and firms which occur in spatial patterns that have meaning in planning for land use". Using Chapin's term we shall in this chapter: first, describe how the physical expression of an activity system comes to be concentrated into a few areas within a town: second, describe how activity systems act on each other, and the locational consequences of that.

INTERACTIONS WITHIN AN ACTIVITY SYSTEM

We shall consider separately four activity systems—shopping, offices, manufacturing industry, housing—and show why each tends to cluster. That is, we shall show why the buildings housing the same activity tend to be located near to each other. For each of the four activity systems, the reasons for clustering can be grouped into two—the need for accessibility, and the desire to enjoy external economies. (External economies are the cost savings to a firm contributed not by the single firm but by other firms in the same industry.) The clustering of one activity system tends, automatically, to exclude other activity systems even though there may be no antipathy between the systems.

Shopping

Accessibility. In Chapter 7 we said that people going shopping want a short and convenient journey. So shopkeepers, in order to capture customers' trade, want a location that is very accessible from residential areas. As there are few such locations within a town, the search for accessibility causes shops to cluster. The place of maximum accessibility in most Western towns which have a pre-motor car structure is the central area, and it is there that the clustering of shops is most evident.

External economies. The gains to shopkeepers from external economies are described by Barrett (1973, p. 80): "In the case of shops, clustering tendencies are mainly in response to consumer behaviour, like-shops tending to come together to offer the customer maximum choice for minimum effort. ... This is obviously of special relevance to shops selling comparison goods, but it should be noted that adjacent shops which appear to be competitive may in fact be complementary because of subtle but significant differences between goods and services offered and type of customer.... Clustering of some shops may be further encouraged by business links between the shopkeepers. Much of an antique dealer's trade, for example, is derived from other antique dealers, and it is facilitated by the tendency towards specialisation within the trade."

In order to understand that better, ask yourself: Where would I go to buy a pair of shoes, when I am not sure what kind I want?

Most people answer: To the High Street, where I may wander in and out of several shops to get the best choice. So if you wanted to sell shoes (and could afford the rents) where would you trade? In the High Street.

Offices

Accessibility. Offices providing personal services (see Chapter 7) need to be accessible to customers, and that leads them to seek sites in city or suburban centres, as do shops. Other types of offices do not provide personal services—e.g. the head offices of manufacturing firms, banking and insurance houses—but they still need accessibility, for a different reason: they need accessibility for their workers. As such offices are often very big, and as there are other strong clustering forces on them (see below), their staffs could not all travel to work by car: the congestion would be too great. So such offices seek locations which are made accessible by public transport. Again, there are few such locations, and the most accessible location is usually the central area. (See, for example, the recent development of offices by London central stations—Cannon Street, Victoria, London Bridge, Euston, etc.)

External economies. The main external economy causing offices to cluster is the need to exchange information between offices. Much of the exchange has to be made face-to-face and at short notice, requiring frequent contact between office workers. Such contacts between offices in London have been investigated by Goddard (1971, 1973).

Manufacturing industry

Accessibility. The needs of manufacturing industry for good accessibility have weakened considerably in the last 20 to 30 years. A firm's workers need to be able to get to work easily, and when those journeys were predominantly by public transport, firms benefitted by being near to public transport nodes, especially the city centre. As more and more people travel to work by car, it is not just that points of high accessibility move (e.g. from the city centre to the suburbs) but that accessibility advantages become dispersed and cease to be concentrated in a few places. (It is interesting to remember that, much earlier, when people walked to work, the need for firms to be very near the workers caused a dispersal of firms—e.g. the cotton mills dispersed throughout residential areas in the old Lancashire textile towns.)

As well as needing labour, a firm needs energy, and when that was supplied by coal (or, earlier, by falling water) the high cost of transporting the energy led to many firms clustering around coal-fields. As more and more firms use gas or oil (which can be transported through pipelines) or electricity (flowing along wires), another clustering tendency is weakened.

Also, a firm wants low transport costs, for its inputs of intermediate goods and of raw materials and for its products. When transport was by rail or water, access to transport was focussed on a few locations, (e.g. the Trafford Park Industrial Estate was served by rail and by the Manchester Ship Canal). Industrial transport is now largely by road, and the road system disperses accessibility advantages widely.

In such ways, the need of manufacturing plants for good accessibility does not cause such plants to cluster together as closely as they once did.

Those arguments do not apply, however, to some firms which manufacture for a localised market with which close contact is essential (e.g. making clothes for fashion-conscious city-centre shops, printing for city-centre offices). In those cases, the need for good accessibility remains, and causes the firms to cluster (in the above examples, near to the city centre. See Edge, 1973). But there is some evidence to show that clothing and printing are starting to decentralise (see Cameron G. C. and Evans, 1973).

External economies. There are some external economies which manufacturing firms may be able to realise if the firms locate near to each other. Let us look at some examples.

Insofar as firms require special roads or engineering services (e.g. high voltage electricity, special waste disposal facilities) those can be provided more cheaply for several firms together than for the same firms separated. Some services for the workers (e.g. cafes, or a health service as on the industrial estate at Harlow New Town) can be provided more cheaply for a group of firms. For example, if a firm locates near other firms, in the vicinity there will probably be private cafes which cater for the work force. If the same firm isolates itself in a suburb, it may have to provide its own canteen. A firm may be able to "sub-contract" part of its work to a specialist firm which, by specialising in one process, can do the job more cheaply. Such specialist sub-contractors are able to find enough custom only by working for several firms. So they locate only by a cluster of firms (e.g. typing agencies, financial and legal services). If such inter-industry links develop, an "industrial complex" arises, such as the jewellery quarter in Birmingham where each firm specialises in one small part of jewellery manufacture. As a result, production costs are reduced. (On how external economies affect manufacturing industry in central areas see Edge, 1973.)

Housing

As housing occupies about 40% of urban land (i.e. houses, gardens, estate roads, local open spaces: see Stone, 1963, chap. 3), there is not the opportunity for it to cluster or disperse, as there is for shopping, offices, or manufacturing industry. Nevertheless, the method of analysis used above can still helpfully be applied to housing. We find that the need for accessibility and the desire for external economies do not lead to housing being clustered within any one city: rather they lead to housing being clustered into a few large towns and cities rather than into many small towns, and they act to stop residential densities falling.

Accessibility. People want to be able to travel easily from their homes to work, to the shops, to school, etc. Such facilities are themselves clustered, so housing tends to locate around such clusters.

External economies. Insofar as households pay for residential roads, for engineering services, for schools, clinics, and other social facilities, it is cheaper for households to locate together. That is because such physical infrastructure and social amenities can be provided more cheaply for a concentrated population than for a dispersed population.

The process of exclusion

If buildings housing the same activity want to cluster together, they can do so only by excluding other activities from the land and buildings in that area. So where there is a desire to cluster, so also there is a locational separation of activities.

How does the process of exclusion work? The shorthand answer is: through the land market. What does that mean? If there is competition for space, so that two different activities want to be on the same site, that activity to which the site is more valuable obtains the site by paying more money for it. The other activity then has to look for another site, one which is more valuable to it than to the first activity, so that the other activity is not outbid again. In that way, activity systems exclude each other and acquire locations in which they can cluster. The process does not work quickly, because the longevity of buildings slows down land use changes, but the process grinds on.

Insofar as all activities want easily accessible locations, and insofar as the central area is the location of maximum accessibility, all activity systems would like to locate in the centre. In that competition for space, who wins? In Western cities, shops and offices usually win because the central location is worth more to them than to any other activity. What do the vanquished do then? It depends on their accessibility needs, and on how accessibility varies throughout the city. In the model concentric Western city, manufacturing industry takes the next most accessible location (the ring around the central area) and housing is excluded from anywhere but the suburbs. (For a simple model of how the exclusion process works in a concentric city see Barrett, 1973.)

We have described how exclusion is achieved by market forces. In Britain, exclusion is achieved also by town planning which zones land for single land uses and so tends to exclude from a plot of land all land uses except one.

INTERACTIONS BETWEEN ACTIVITY SYSTEMS

Two types of interaction between activity systems have already been discussed: *attraction* and *exclusion*. Attraction is when the need for accessibility leads activity systems to locate near to each other (e.g. the spatial interaction theories of shopping location, described in Chapter 7, emphasised the benefits to be gained by shops in being near to houses). Exclusion has just been described, the passive exclusion by one activity system of all other activity systems from a desired location. There is a third type of interaction—*segregation* of activity systems from each other. "Exclusion drives uses away ... but segregation drives groups of uses apart ... ", says Vance (1971, p. 115). Whereas exclusion is passive, segregation is active: there is a definite antipathy between activity systems. Two important cases of segregation are described below.

Housing and industry

Most people do not want to live near to manufacturing industry, disliking the noise, sight, traffic and (where applicable) the fumes caused by factories. It may be that such dislike of industry stems from earlier times when industry was much dirtier and noisier (and it has been suggested that modern industry makes a good neighbour—see *Man Plan 3: Town Workshop*, 1969). Moreover, the value to working mothers of small pockets of industry within residential areas should be remembered (see Chapter 6). Nevertheless, people still want to live away from industry in nice, quiet, wholly residential, suburbs (and various attempts are being made to measure the money value of that desire: see, for example Davies, 1973).

Shopping and other uses

Shopkeepers believe that a continuous and unbroken shopping frontage is necessary for high sales in their shops, because a break in the shopping frontage (e.g. by offices, estate agents, garages, houses) reduces the attractiveness of the street to shoppers. In spite of the absence of hard evidence with which to support that belief, shopkeepers, shopping developers, and often town planners try actively to keep other uses out of shopping streets.

For examples of the attempt to enforce the segregation of shops, see Multiple Shops Federation (1963, para. 60), and your local paper. There you will see reports of planning applications to change the use of buildings in shopping streets from shops to offices for insurance brokers, building societies, travel agents, estate agents, and the like. Often the planning department refuses the applications, one of the reasons being that the continuous shopping frontage of an established shopping street would be broken. Sometimes the cases go to appeal: that is when they enter the local newspapers. Also, there are examples of big shopping companies buying vacant shops in areas where the companies have valuable stores, in order to prevent the vacant buildings being acquired for non-shopping uses.

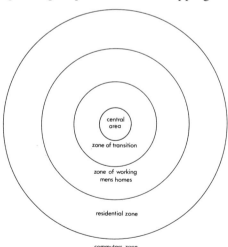

Fig. 8.1. Burgess's diagram of city ecology.

FUNCTIONAL AREAS

The locational result of the interactions within, and between activity systems is the development of *functional areas*, areas in each
one of which an activity system is concentrated. These functional
areas can be described in terms of broad urban zones (as, for
example, Burgess's famous diagram of city ecology, see Fig. 8.1), or

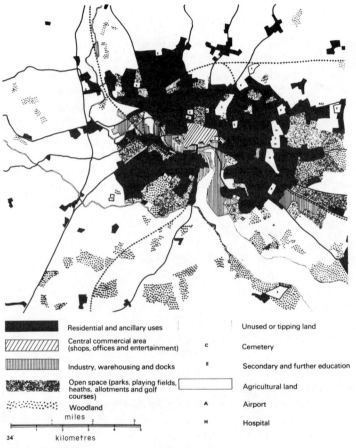

▰ Residential and ancillary uses		Unused or tipping land
▨ Central commercial area (shops, offices and entertainment)	C	Cemetery
▥ Industry, warehousing and docks	E	Secondary and further education
▦ Open space (parks, playing fields, heaths, allotments and golf courses)	▢	Agricultural land
⋯ Woodland	A	Airport
	H	Hospital

miles

kilometres

Fig. 8.2. Land uses in Ipswich (from Ipswich Draft Basic Plan, 1968,
by courtesy of H.M.S.O.).

land uses, where each activity system requires a different land use (see Figs. 8.2, and 8.3), or detailed activity differences within one land use (see Fig. 8.4). (For examples of differences within residential areas, see Chapter 9.)

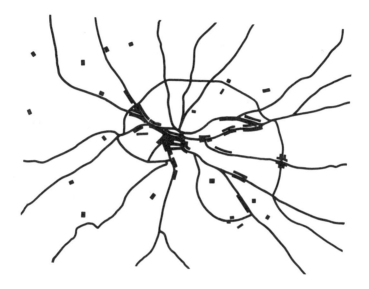

Fig. 8.3. The location of shops in Ipswich (from Ipswich Draft Basic Plan, 1968, by courtesy of H.M.S.O.).

INTERACTIONS BETWEEN FUNCTIONAL AREAS

The forces which lead activity systems to cluster and so create functional areas have been described. And three types of interaction between activity systems have been described—attraction, exclusion and segregation. So it is apparent that if one activity system changes, that may cause changes in other activity systems. Where those changes have locational effects, it is convenient to consider them as being interactions between functional areas. Some examples of such interactions are described below.

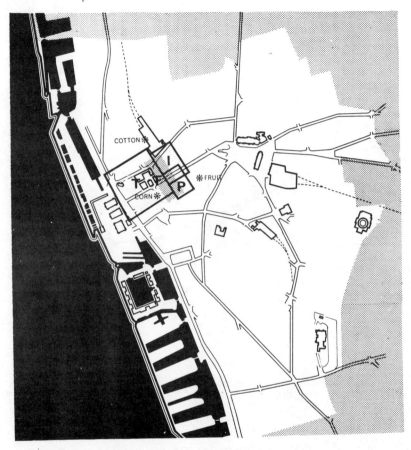

Fig. 8.4. The office quarter in Liverpool central area (from Liverpool City Centre Plan, by courtesy of the City of Liverpool). I, Insurance; T, Transport; P, Professions. *Commodity exchanges.

The central area and the inner ring

Burgess's concentric model of urban structure (Burgess, 1925: also see Fig. 8.1) is a dynamic model applicable to a growing city. In that city, the central area retains its attraction for shops, offices, and industry, so as the city grows more such activities seek a central location. They can achieve it only by excluding other activities in or on the edge of the central area. For historical reasons, the land use which is in that position and which is most easily displaced is housing. So shops, offices, and industry try to expand in the centre: the extra shops get the most central sites, thus displacing offices and industry: the new and the displaced offices and industry expand into the inner ring, thus displacing housing.

That change takes time, and the houses in the inner ring are not demolished and replaced by offices and factories as soon as the households move out. The reason is that the housing structures still have a lot of economic life left in them, so it would be too expensive to demolish them. Moreover the offices and industries which are displaced into the inner ring are likely to be the poorer firms which lost the fight to stay in the centre, so such firms are least able to afford to demolish and rebuild. As a result, houses become used for offices and industry. Houses remaining in residential use therefore have an uncertain future, so their owners do not maintain them: richer residents move out, poorer residents move in at higher occupancy rates, and the housing deteriorates physically.

So it is that Burgess calls the inner ring the "zone in transition" (although it is not clear why: in his theory all zones are in transition). He observed it in Chicago in the 1920's, we observe it in Britain today: Edge (1973) describes the conversion of houses, church halls, etc. in Balsall Heath (within Birmingham's inner ring) for small firms forced out of the centre of Birmingham, not by the expansion of shops and offices but by planned urban renewal.

Housing and shopping

If shops are in the city centre, if people want to live near to shops, and if residential areas start to spread out from the city centre, then more and more people come to live in an inconvenient location for shopping. What happens then?

Barrett (1973, p. 101) provides the answer. "The (second) main factor in central business district decline is the changing residential pattern. While population at the urban margin increases through ever

TABLE 8.1. THE CENTRAL AREA'S SHARE IN THE CITY'S TOTAL SHOPPING
TRADE (U.S.)

Population of city	Share of retail business in central business district
0–25,000	80–100%
25,000–100,000	65–85%
100,000–400,000	50–70%
400,000–750,000	30–55%
Over 750,000	15–35%

Source: Smith, L., 1971.
Note: For a British comparison, in Birmingham with a population of around one million, the city centre takes about 25% of the total retail business in the city (City of Birmingham Structure Plan, 1973).

expanding urban sprawl, the population of the inner residential zone adjacent to the central business district decreases. More and more people are living further and further away from the central business district. Population means purchasing power, and this shift in purchasing power to the suburbs is all the more pronounced as the inner zone becomes increasingly dominated by lower income groups."

So a smaller proportion of shopping is transacted in the city centre as residential areas spread outwards. One manifestation of that is the share of retail expenditure taken by the central business district related to city size, for which we have some American data (Table 8.1).

It is not just the total amounts and locations of housing and shopping which are related: also there is a relationship between the type of people living in the houses and the type of shops. Rich people have more money to spend in shops than poor people, but also have different tastes from poor people. So they demand, and get, different types of shops. If poor people live on the east side of the city and rich people on the west, the poorer shopping will be on the east and the better on the west: that relationship is very clear in London. And if the types of people living in an area change, then so do the types of shops serving that area. That can be seen around Notting Hill Gate in London: as the housing was being converted from family dwellings into bedsitters, so ironmongers, family grocers, and chemists gave way to laundromats, Sunday-opening supermarkets, and employment bureaus.

Housing and industry

Just as shops want to be near the housing which accommodates their customers, so industry wants to be near the housing which accommodates its workers. We explained earlier how, in a traditional concentric city, the location most accessible for workers was the central area. However, as the population of a city grows, so it spreads outwards and away from the centre: moreover the inner-ring suburbs lose population absolutely as well as relatively. (The City of Birmingham Structure Plan, 1973, Report on Population, Fig. 3, shows that for Birmingham, and the picture is similar in most big towns.) So we expect industry to move as, in the same conditions, shopping has moved—to the suburbs. Surburbanisation of industry is, indeed, what we observe (see Edge, 1973, and Pred, 1971). Cameron and Evans (1973, p. 50) have measured the movement between 1961 and 1966, for six conurbation centres, and state: "In many cases, the falls in employment in manufacturing and wholesaling were very large, both absolutely and proportionately, given that we are considering a period of only five years. These changes in the employment structures of the conurbation centres have resulted ... because conurbation employment has become less and less concentrated in the conurbation centres."

One of the reasons for the suburbanisation of industry is the suburbanisation of population, as suggested above. Edge (1973, p. 135) discusses empirical evidence: "(Factory owners in Toronto) argued that most of their employees, prior to the firm relocating, lived in the same sector of the city as the one in which they worked. However, their homes were located further out from the city centre than was their workplace.... Managers argued that by relocating a factory in the same sector of the city but at a greater distance from the central business district they actually moved the workplace nearer to the workers and thus lost no valuable employees.... The supply of female labour was also mentioned as one of the attractions of a suburban industrial location." Reporting another empirical survey, Cameron and Johnson (1969) state that clothing manufacturers in central Glasgow opened branch factories in the suburbs because they could not obtain in the city centre the workers necessary for expanding production. Keeble and Hauser (1971 and 72) report the rapid growth of manufacturing employment in the South East beyond Greater London, and link that growth to the availability of labour there.

The central area and industry

Another reason for the suburbanisation of industry is the growth of other activities in the central area. The growing activities are mainly shops and offices, to which central area land is more valuable than to industry, so industry is excluded from the centre by the operation of the land market. Reviewing empirical studies, Edge (1973) shows that the shortage of land at acceptable prices is one of the two most important forces pushing industry out of city centres.

Housing and offices

People who work in offices tend to be of a social and occupational status different from the national average, and such occupational and social groups often live in housing areas segregated from other status groups (see Chapter 9). If one of the locational forces on offices was the desire to be located conveniently for their staff, we would expect to find offices located in, and moving into, areas near where office workers live. Casual observation confirms this, such as the growth of offices in the West End of London rather than the East End, and the movement of offices out of London to Croydon, out of Manchester to Wilmslow, and out of Birmingham to Solihull (Smith, 1974).

INDEX TO REFERENCES IN CHAPTER 8

BARRETT, J., 1973, "The form and functions of the central area", in *The City as an Economic System*, The Open University Press, Bletchley.
BURGESS, E. W., 1925, "The growth of the city", in Park, R. E. *et al.*, *The City*, University of Chicago Press.

CAMERON, G. C. and EVANS, A. W., 1973, "The British conurbation centres", *Regional Studies*, vol. 7, no. 1.

CAMERON, G. C. and JOHNSON, K. M., 1969, "Urban renewal and industrial location", in Cullingworth, J. B. and Orr, S. C. (eds.), *Regional and Urban Studies*, Allen & Unwin, London.

CHAPIN, F. S., 1965, *Urban Land-Use Planning*, University of Illinois, 2nd ed.

"City of Birmingham Structure Plan", 1973, Birmingham.

DAVIES, G. J., 1973, "An econometric model of residential amenity", papers of the 1973 Urban Economics Conference, Centre for Environmental Studies, London.

EDGE, G., 1973, "The suburbanisation of industry", in *The City as an Economic System*, The Open University Press, Bletchley.

GODDARD, J. B., 1971, "Office communications and office location", *Regional Studies*, vol. 5, no. 4.

GODDARD, J. B., 1973, "Information flows and the development of the Urban System", papers of the 1973 Urban Economics Conference, Centre for Environmental Studies, London.

KEEBLE, D. E. and HAUSER, D. P., 1971 and 1972, "Manufacturing growth in South East England", *Regional Studies*, vol. 5, no. 4; vol. 6, no. 1.

"Man Plan 3: Town Workshop", 1969, *The Architectural Review*, vol. 146, no. 873.

Multiple Shops Federation, 1963, *The Planning of Shopping Centres*, London.

PRED, A. R., 1971, "The intra-metropolitan location of American manufacturing", in Bourne, L. S. (ed.), *Internal Structure of the City*, OUP, New York.

SMITH, B. M. D., 1974, "Employment opportunities in the Inner Area Study part of Small Heath Birmingham in 1974", Research Memorandum no. 38, CURS, University of Birmingham.

SMITH, L., 1971, "Space for the CBD's functions" in Bourne, L. S. (ed.), *Internal Structure of the City*, OUP, New York.

STONE, P. A., 1963, "Housing, Town Development, Land and Costs", *The Estates Gazette*, London.

VANCE, J. E., 1971, "Focus on downtown", in Bourne, L. S. (ed.), *Internal Structure of the City*, OUP, New York.

FURTHER READING FOR CHAPTER 8

BERRY, B. J. L. and HORTON, F. E., 1970, *Geographic Perspectives on Urban Systems*, Prentice Hall, New Jersey, chapter 12.

BOURNE, L. S. (ed.), 1971, *Internal Structure of the City*, OUP, New York, parts II, IV, and VI.

CARTER, H., 1972, *The Study of Urban Geography*, Arnold, London, chapters 9, 10, 13.

DANIELS, P. W., 1975, *Office Location*, Bell, London.

GOODALL, B., 1972, *The Economics of Urban Areas*, Pergamon, Oxford, chapters 4, 5, 6, 7, 8.

JOHNSON, J. H., 1967, *Urban Geography*, Pergamon, Oxford, chapters 6, 7, 8, 9.

PATERSON, J. H., 1972, *Land, Work, and Resources*, Arnold, London, chapters 4, 5, 8, 9.

The City as an Economic system, 1973, Open University Press, Bletchley (DT 201, 10–14).

CHAPTER 9

Interactions between Social Groups, House Types, and House Locations

INTRODUCTION

In Chapter 8 we saw that houses tend to cluster together and not to mix with other land uses. We know also that there is clustering within housing as a land use, and that we take as the subject of this chapter. This clustering can be analysed both in terms of the *social characteristics* of the households and in terms of the *housing characteristics* of the dwellings.

If we look at social characteristics we find that people of similar ages tend to live near to each other and apart from people of different ages, and we find this for other social characteristics too, such as income, occupation, race, religion. That type of clustering can be called *social grouping* (and it is, of course, the same as social segregation by place of residence). Looking at housing characteristics we find dwellings clustered by age, by tenure, by size, by structural condition, by provision of amenities such as running water, and so on. We shall call that type of clustering *housing grouping*.

Moreover, we often find that social grouping and housing grouping are inter-related: that is, where there is a social grouping of households with particular social characteristics (e.g. high income, high status) the households are living in a housing grouping of dwellings with particular housing characteristics (e.g. big, owner-occupied, good structural condition). The geographical area where a social grouping and a housing grouping coincide we shall call a *housing area*.

108

In this chapter we want to explain why social grouping, housing grouping, and housing areas occur, the location of housing areas, and how housing areas interact. Our explanations will be in terms of the interactions between social groups, house types, and house locations. Those interactions form what has been called the *socio-eco-logical system* (Pahl, 1968 (a), p. 10), and the explanations which we want should be provided by theories of that system. The search for a theory of the socio-ecological system started in the 1920's with the Chicago school, and Burgess's concentric zone theory (Burgess, 1925) is the best-known product of that school (see Fig. 8.1). The Chicago approach has been shown to be no longer helpful, and several recent theories compete to displace the Chicago school. Some of the newer theories are described later in this chapter, but none is so well developed that it can convincingly offer us the explanations that we want. For that reason, the explanations given here of social grouping, housing grouping, and housing areas are partial and tentative.

It may be helpful to describe the relationship of this chapter to Chapter 5, which was also about people and housing. Here, the analysis of Chapter 5 is taken further in four ways: we consider what happens when the housing demands of one household are not independent of the housing demands of other households (i.e. the economist's assumption of independent demands is dropped); we introduce location into the analysis of both housing demand and housing supply; we analyse housing submarkets in terms of the social characteristics of households; and we approach housing demand from the direction of the constraints on a household as well as from the direction of choice. Nevertheless, the fundamental method of Chapter 5—the supply and demand approach—is retained throughout this present chapter.

To end this introduction, let us see some examples of social grouping, housing grouping, and housing areas. Social grouping can be easily shown on simple maps: Figs. 9.1 and 9.2 show social grouping by age and by socio-economic group for Birmingham. Housing grouping can be shown in the same way: Figs. 9.3 and 9.4 show housing grouping by age of dwelling and by tenure for Birmingham. To detect housing areas is more difficult, because we are looking

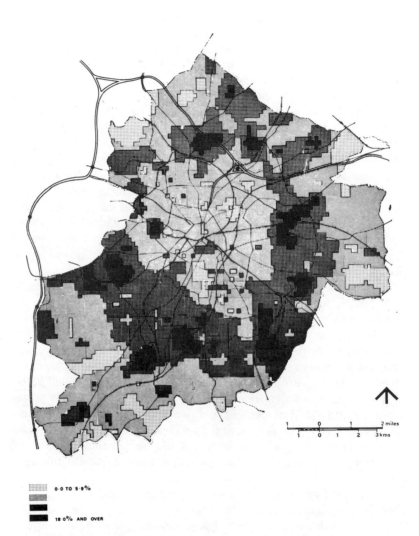

Fig. 9.1. The proportion of the population aged 65 and over, by residential location, Birmingham 1966 (from City of Birmingham Structure Plan, 1973, by courtesy of the City of Birmingham).

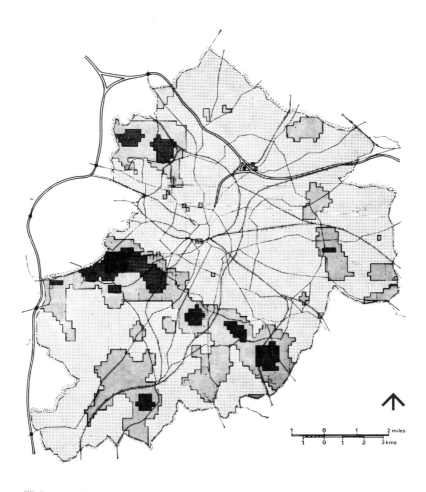

0·0 TO 9·9%

30·0% AND OVER

Fig. 9.2. The proportion of males who are employers and managers, by residential location, Birmingham 1966 (from City of Birmingham Structure Plan, 1973, by courtesy of the City of Birmingham).

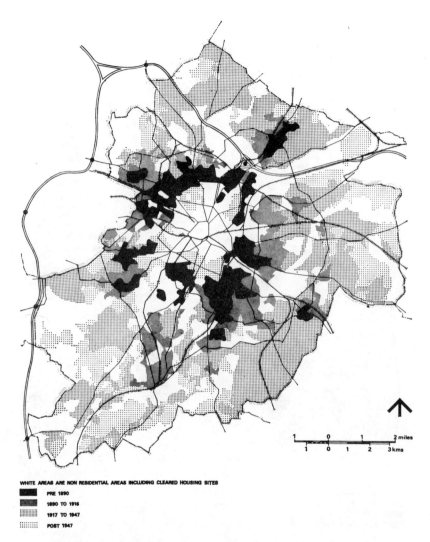

WHITE AREAS ARE NON RESIDENTIAL AREAS INCLUDING CLEARED HOUSING SITES

- PRE 1890
- 1890 TO 1916
- 1917 TO 1947
- POST 1947

Fig. 9.3. Age of dwellings, by location, Birmingham 1972 (from City of Birmingham Structure Plan, 1973, by courtesy of the City of Birmingham).

0·0 TO 24·9%
25·0% TO 49·9%
50·0% TO 74·9%
75·0% AND OVER

Fig. 9.4. The proportion of dwellings rented from the local authority, by location, Birmingham 1966 (from City of Birmingham Structure Plan, 1973, by courtesy of the City of Birmingham).

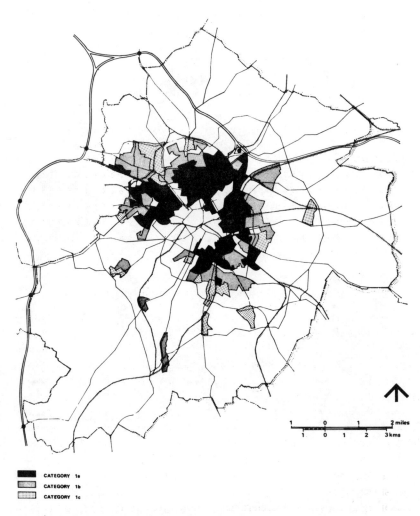

CATEGORY 1a
CATEGORY 1b
CATEGORY 1c

Fig. 9.5. Cluster analysis, Birmingham, 1966 (from City of Birmingham
Structure Plan, 1973, by courtesy of the City of Birmingham).

for a coincidence of social characteristics and housing characteristics in the same location. Two methods that can be used to detect that are social area analysis (see, for example, Murdie, 1971, and Robson, 1969) and cluster analysis. The latter technique was used to produce Fig. 9.5: the map shows areas where poor dwellings and households in difficult circumstances co-exist (in categories 1b and 1c the housing is not as bad as in category 1a).

HOUSING DEMAND AND HOUSING SUPPLY

In this section we take a supply and demand approach to the task of explaining social grouping, housing grouping, and housing areas, and we find that the approach takes us a long way to the goal of a theory of the socio-ecological system. In the introduction of Chapter 5 it was explained that "supply" and "demand" would be used without the precise meanings given to those words in economic theory: it is the same in this chapter.

Demand: the preference for neighbours of one's own type

People may want to live in the same area as other households with similar social characteristics for various reasons. Kirwan and Ball (1973) suggest the following reasons: the external effects of neighbours on the physical environment creating a desired environmental quality; snob effects; a feeling of identity and of being "at home" in a locality with neighbours similar to oneself; proximity to friends and relatives and easy contact with peers; availability and quality of local schools; making more easy the difficult choice of residential location by following the example of peers; a reduced risk of undesired environmental change in the locality.

It has been shown that, if such a preference for neighbours of a similar type is present, it can lead to a high degree of social segregation even though the preference is moderate. Muth (1969) postulates a "consumer preference hypothesis", the hypothesis that whites have a greater aversion to living among negroes than do other negroes. As a result, whites are prepared to offer more for housing in white neighbourhoods than are negroes. The consequence is racially segregated housing areas. Schelling (1971) shows that even without price differences people can move to achieve neighbours similar to themselves, and he shows with some simple games how a moderate desire for similar neighbours can cause social segregation far more complete than most of the persons would want.

Demand: the desire for access

Every house has a particular location relative to shops, workplaces, parks, schools, etc. That is to say, every house offers a "set of accesses" to the urban facilities which the household might want to visit.

Usually, a household's desire for access has been analysed in terms of access to work only: moreover, the assumptions are often made that all workplaces are in the city centre and that all workers want to reduce the money cost of the work journey (see, for example, Kirwan and Ball, 1973). However, workplaces are usually scattered throughout the city, the types of jobs offered in one area of the city (e.g. the centre) may be different from the types of jobs offered in another area (e.g. an industrial estate on the edge of the town), and different people require different things of their work journeys (e.g. a bus driver working the early morning shift wants to live near the bus garage, a teacher may be able always to travel out of the rush-hour). Moreover, access to work is irrelevant to households containing no workers: for retired people, the accessibility of the post office might be the most important consideration.

What that means is that different households want different "sets of accesses" from the locations of their houses. And as different houses offer different "sets of accesses", it is quite possible that the desire for access alone could cause social grouping.

Demand: the desire for housing characteristics

Different houses have different housing characteristics (tenure, size, amenities, etc.). It is often assumed that dwellings can be graded on the basis of their characteristics from the least desirable dwelling to the most desirable, and that all households grade dwellings in the same way. If that were true, what is the most desirable to one household would be the most desirable to all households (Rex, 1968, in his theory described below assumes that explicitly). But the assumption might be wrong, and different households might have different demands for housing characteristics. If houses are clustered by housing characteristics (see below), those differing demands could lead to social grouping.

Supply: housing characteristics

We must remember that by far the largest part of housing supply is from the existing stock of housing: new houses add to the stock only very slowly (see Chapter 5). Now, when houses are built, they are built with certain housing characteristics (size, provision of amenities, density, etc.), and usually the characteristics do not change over the life of the building. (True, some dwellings are converted or improved during their lives, and the number of such conversions is high at present—361,000 in England and Wales in 1973: Housing and Construction Statistics 1974. But before the 1969 Housing Act, conversions were few.) As a result, the supply of houses with particular housing characteristics can be understood by looking at the stock of existing houses and the conditions in which those houses were built.

The economics of house-building are such that a single house is cheaper to build if it is built in an estate with similar houses. As Kirwan and Ball (1973, p. 15) put it, "Indivisibilities and economies of scale will tend to result in houses with similar attributes being built in an area". Moreover (as those authors go on to say) "Land cannot usually be purchased in single lot sites, which encourages the building of groups of houses. Planning regulations tend to increase this indivisibility of land for new building...".

So there are strong supply reasons why houses are often built in big estates of similar houses—i.e. in housing groupings. (There may be demand reasons also—housing developers know of the desire of people to live near to others with similar social characteristics— but we cannot introduce that here without begging the question we are trying to answer.) Some variety of house types may be introduced later to the estates, by infilling or by the redevelopment of old houses with higher density housing, but the affect of such changes on most housing groups is likely to be small.

Supply and demand: social grouping and housing areas

Now we can start to deduce the consequences of connections between the demand to live near people of one's own type, the demand for access, the demand for housing characteristics, and the supply of housing characteristics.

The demand to live near people of one's own type might, on its own, lead to social grouping. (Those are the conditions with which Schelling experimented—see above. Households were indifferent about housing characteristics and accesses.) But that demand on its own will not lead to housing areas: housing will not necessarily be similar within the area of a social grouping. The demand for access also might, on its own, lead to social grouping: that would happen if the demand for access varied with the social characteristics of households. Again, the social grouping would not necessarily be a housing area also. If there is a demand for housing characteristics which varies with the social characteristics of households, and if the supply of housing is in housing groupings, those two conditions alone will cause not only social grouping but also housing areas.

The study of those few possibilities shows that the supply and demand method can offer explanations of the existence of social grouping, housing grouping and housing areas.

Supply and demand: the question of location

One important component of the socio-ecological system which we have not yet considered is the question of location: how are housing areas located with respect to each other and to the city structure? Can the supply and demand approach help us to answer that question?

The usual assumption about housing *demand* is that all households want to live as near to their workplaces as possible, and that the

further away they are the less they are prepared to pay for housing—
i.e. households substitute between transport costs and rent costs (see,
for example, Wingo, 1961, Muth, 1969, and Evans, 1973). Pahl (1965)
is one of the few people to question that assumption explicitly, as
he has to when explaining expensive commuter villages in the metropolitan fringe (see Chapter 4). (For a good discussion of the demand
for residential location see Richardson, 1971.) Hoyt (1939) made the
different assumption that rich households demand to live near to
each other (but on a good route to the city centre), that middle-
income households demand to live near to rich households, and that
poor people live in the areas remaining. That led him to predict
a radial sector theory of housing areas.

Assumptions about the location of housing *supply* are usually less
explicit. Often it is implied that the historical conditions of the
growth of the city determine the location of housing groupings. For
example, in mediaeval times the merchants lived in the city centre
and the poor on the outskirts. Then there was a rapid growth of
working-class housing around the city centre. Then middle-class
suburbs were built. Then richer commuter areas were developed.
Hence, the newer the housing, the further it is from the centre, and
the better it is physically. (That is the locational basis of Burgess's
concentric theory of urban structure—Burgess, 1925—and of Rex's
theory described below.) There might be special supply conditions
which modify the above process. For example, in Britain, the prevail-
ing wind from the west blows the city centre smoke to the east,
making the east unattractive to, and therefore shunned by, rich
people (see Mann, 1965).

That short survey shows that the supply and demand approach
can help to explain the location of housing areas, but that it cannot
give complete explanations. For that we need more knowledge of
the interactions between the supply of and demand for housing.

THE ALLOCATION OF SUPPLY AMONG DEMANDERS

The outcome of the interaction between supply and demand
depends on the nature of the interaction process. (See the section

on housing markets in Chapter 5: the response of supply to a housing demand depends on whether that demand is expressed in the private housing market or the public housing market.)

Is housing allocated *through the market*? If so, then households bid against each other for dwellings, and any contested dwelling goes to the household which offers most money. And dwellings are supplied in response to the money demand which reveals itself through that market process. Is there *discrimination* against some households, which affects the market process? By that we do not mean: do some social groups choose to live away from other social groups? but: is there a refusal to supply some types of housing, or housing in some locations, to certain social groups? (See, for example, the laws which existed in some states of America, laws which were deliberately designed to maintain residential segregation based on race.)

Are there *institutional procedures* which restrict demand, not procedures which help the impersonal market to work better by oiling its wheels, but procedures which work arbitrarily in terms of market efficiency? For example, your demand for local authority housing might be ineffective until you have lived in the district for 3 years, or you might not get a 90% mortgage if you have a manual job. (Barbolet, 1969, found that manual workers could not obtain mortgages as big as those obtained by non-manual workers with the same incomes.)

When people demand housing, how much effective *choice* do they have and what are the *constraints* on their choice? Is a household's choice limited only by its income? If so, how much choice has a poor household? Or is choice further limited by discrimination and institutional procedures? If so, do some households have no effective choice? The answers, of course, will probably vary greatly with the economic and social status of households: as Harvey says "... the rich can command space whereas the poor are trapped in it" (Harvey, 1971, p. 171). Pahl (1968(b)), wanting to develop theory which will help social policy, recommends a constraints approach. "I think we should concern ourselves with understanding the constraints and let the choices look after themselves. Surely the whole point about a mixed economy is that it is only partly planned" (p. 20). Theory for other purposes, however, may best be pursued using both a choice and a constraints approach.

All those unanswered questions, and many others, indicate that there is no one accepted explanation of the location of housing areas. So we shall look at several theories which give competing explanations.

SOME THEORIES OF THE SOCIO-ECOLOGICAL SYSTEM

The interactions between social groups, house types, and house locations constitute the socio-ecological system. All the theories of that system which we shall describe take the supply and demand approach (as we have defined it), and we shall see that the differences between the theories are of two types. First there are differences in the *process* by which supply and demand interact, the process of housing allocation. Second there are differences in *initial conditions*, the geographical and historical conditions on which the processes operate.

Burgess's theory of urban zones

We shall start with this theory (Burgess, 1925), because it is the oldest and best known. But there is not much theory to describe. "In the expansion of the city a process of distribution takes place which sifts and sorts and relocates individuals and groups, by residence and occupation" says Burgess (p. 54, 1967 impression), but how that happens is not described. The process of interaction between social groups, house types, and house locations is "competition for land use", and the locational process is one of "domination, invasion, and succession" through urban zones, the locations of which are determined by historical supply conditions. The process can best be described as a *private-market* process for allocating land and houses; the competition for land use is an economic competition.

Rent theories

A variant of the private-market allocation process is suggested by rent theories. The variation is that, instead of continuous competitive

bidding for land between rich and poor, there is a sequential allocation, with the rich getting the first choice. (Hoyt's theory—see
above—is clearly an early example.) Harvey calls such theories
"space-packing models" (Harvey, 1973, p. 172).

Rent theories say that all people want to be near the centre of
the city, because there their transport costs are lowest. The more
people spend on transport, the less they can spend on housing. Rich
people can always afford to pay more for housing land than can
poor people, and the amount they can pay declines only slowly with
distance from the centre. In Western cities, rich people's preference
for space leads them to live on the outskirts, leaving the city centres
for poor people: as land is expensive there, the poor people must
live at high densities. In some Indian and Latin American cities,
rich people prefer city centre living; then poor people must live on
the outskirts, where land is cheaper but transport costs much higher,
and they may have to walk to work.

The other theories of the socio-ecological system to be described
below reject the assumption that housing and housing land are
always allocated in a private market.

The social ecology of Prague

Musil (1968) criticises the private-market theory by showing that
it no longer applies to Prague. "During the two post-war decades,
an important change has taken place, which can be described generally as a trend towards the evening-out of the differences between
the ... zones. ... There are two main causes for this development
towards greater homogeneity. The first one is connected with the
control of Prague's growth, the second one with the transformation
of the nature of the ecological processes which operate within
Czechoslovak cities" (p. 256). The transformation is in the way housing is allocated: allocation is no longer through the market. As a
result, " ... the land values and the rents are almost irrelevant to
the distribution of socio-economic groups of population" (p. 257).

Musil goes on to describe the new allocation process—"a housing
policy which allocates new dwellings by preference to young families
with children, to employees of key economic branches, and to families

living in very bad and unhealthy dwellings" (p. 258)—but he does not try to elevate that into a new general theory of the socio-ecological system.

The city of socialist man

Fisher (1962) describes another situation in which the private market does not operate and in which the process of housing allocation is political rather than economic. The official aim is to devise an allocation method which will produce classless and unsegrated housing areas.

What has happened in those socialist countries which have tried to implement that ideology? asks Fisher. He finds that there is one type of segregation forced on socialist planners by the housing shortage and economic scarcity: segregation by household size. That is the result of building and allocating dwellings strictly according to the size of households which will occupy them, and of building estates of single person dwellings, of two-person dwellings, etc.

Fisher finds also segregation by social characteristics, a contradiction of the ideology. But the segregation is not that of Western cities, where market forces allocate the most desirable houses to the richest: rather it is the result of political forces and of the necessity to give "pay-offs to select groups". Who are the groups with special abilities required by the state? "The first-class residential areas do not now belong to the capitalists, but to the Party and to the government and industrial élite."

The theory of housing classes

Rex (1968) puts forward a theory of the socio-ecological system which he applies to present-day British cities (without claiming that it can be applied more generally). The housing allocation process involves both market and political forces, and the initial conditions are historically determined situations of housing supply and housing attitudes.

The present *housing supply* derives from "the sort of industrial settlement with its civic facilities which grew up in England in the

19th century"—the homes of the upper middle-class near the city centre, and grid-iron rows of working-class cottages. "Gradually, however, and particularly during the period between 1880 and 1914, a third way of life began to emerge between these two. It was the way of life of growing numbers of white-collar people." Their houses were built in the city's inner ring. "In the 20th century, however, the great urban game of leapfrog begins." That produces three ways of life and housing: the richest settle in the "classy inner suburbs"; the white-collar people, aided by mortages, live further out in semi-detached suburbs; "and, finally, the working classes, having attained a measure of power in the city hall, have their own suburbs built for them."

The present *housing attitudes* consider those three ways of life and housing desirable and normal. "Less desirable or less normal is the way of life of those who now inhabit the inner zone." And for almost all households, surburban housing is a desired resource, although it is in scarce supply.

The basic *process* in the socio-ecological system is "competition for scarce and desired types of housing. In this process, people are distinguished from one another by their strength in . . . the system of housing allocation". Rex suggests that there are in modern British cities seven *housing classes*, ranked in order of their strength in the system:

> the outright owners of large houses in desirable areas;
> mortgage payers who "own" whole houses in desirable areas;
> council tenants in council-built houses;
> council tenants in slum houses awaiting demolition;
> tenants of private house-owners, usually in the inner ring;
> house owners who must take lodgers to meet loan repayments;
> lodgers in rooms (Rex, 1968, pp. 212–15).

Rex has applied the theory of housing classes to a particular type of area (a zone of transition) and where there are racial complications (Rex and Moore, 1967). Pahl (1970) has shown that the general theory but with different housing classes can be applied also to a commuter village.

INTERACTION BETWEEN HOUSING AREAS

We have tried above to explain how there arise housing areas—geographical areas in which the social characteristics of households are similar and the housing characteristics of dwellings are similar. And from the way in which those areas arise (more accurately, the way in which different theories suggest that they arise) we can deduce that the housing areas within any one city are not independent of one another. So we can predict that, if one housing area changes, that will cause other housing areas to change. Below we give some suggestions about how that happens and some examples of how it actually happens.

Burgess's theory of city growth

"The main fact of expansion", says Burgess (p. 50, 1967 impression), is "the tendency of each inner zone to extend its area by the invasion of the next outer zone." So, if a city is growing, adjacent housing areas interact in that way.

The effects of slum clearance

In Birmingham, slums are mostly small privately-rented dwellings. What is likely to happen when housing areas are cleared? "The inevitable consequences", according to Rex and Moore (1967, p. 27), are, "a decline in the number of small family cottages available for letting, and a decline in the proportion of privately owned rented housing. It is thus inevitable that the housing of those for whom the council cannot provide will fall more and more to the owners and owner-occupiers of large houses. Where there is both a slum-clearance programme and a long-unsatisfied council waiting-list, the pressure for accommodation in large houses which are not slums is bound to grow."

Such consequences of slum clearance on other housing areas are not new: Dyos (1961) reports how in the second half of the 19th century Camberwell and Peckham had to accommodate families displaced by improvement schemes which affected their homes in central London.

Intra-urban migration

Blair (1969) suggests that there are three broad housing markets: home owners in the property owning democracy (PODs, 48% of households in 1966), poor insecure tenants (PITs) of private landlords (21% of households in 1966), and residents of council housing (welfstaters, 26% in 1966). Most residents stay within their own housing market, but there is some movement: élite PITs become PODs and welfstaters, but few families move between the Welfstat and POD sectors. Houses in a particular market tend to be in a particular

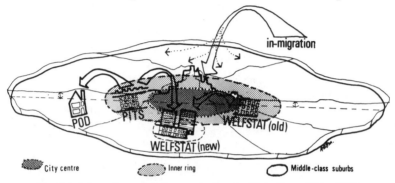

Fig. 9.6. Intra-urban migration, according to Blair (from Blair, 1969, Social systems analysis, *Official Architecture and Planning*, Vol. 32, by courtesy of Architecture and Planning Publications Ltd.).

part of the city—i.e. in housing areas—so movements between market sectors are also movements between housing areas. For example, if dwellings are taken out of the PIT sector (by, for example, the gentrification of inner ring housing), the élite PITs will join the PODs in their suburbs or the welfstaters in their separate suburbs, and the remaining PITs will try to join other PITs in the inner ring. Blair illustrates that with a diagram (see Fig. 9.6).

The filtering process

That is the name given to the process by which households move between house types, where the house types are classified by price (e.g. out of a poor, cheap house into a better, more expensive house).

How the process is supposed to work is illustrated by the following example. Suppose the number of rich households is fixed. Then some expensive dwellings are built. Some of the rich households move into those new dwellings, vacating their previous dwellings. The good dwellings thus vacated fall in price (relatively if not absolutely) and are bought by less rich households. Those vacate less good dwellings which are then occupied by those on the next lowest rung of the housing market. That process continues until some of those worst housed move into slightly better housing. In that way, the provision of expensive housing improves the quality of the housing stock, and the improvement "filters" through the housing market so that even those most badly housed get some of the improvement.

That is the theory. And it is a comforting theory because the provision of even very expensive houses can be justified socially on the grounds that it will improve housing conditions for the poorest people. Is it a correct theory? A recent empirical study in Scotland (Watson, 1973) shows that new building does create a chain of household movement: for every 1000 new owner-occupied dwellings built, 2090 households were able to move, and for every 1000 new local authority dwellings, 1640 households were able to move. Moreover, most of the moves were "upward": households moved into better accommodation as a result of the new building. However, filtering is not an efficient way of helping those in housing need: "...policies...could be devised so that particular groups in the population can be helped directly, without having to rely on the indirect 'trickle down' of benefits from the programme of new building" (p. 54).

The blow-out theory

Harvey suggests this as an alternative to the filter-down theory: instead of improvements to good housing filtering down to poor people, poor people can get richer people to vacate good housing. "The poorest groups, who have the greatest latent demand for housing and the least resources to procure it, cannot afford new housing. Yet poor groups have a singular power (a power which many of them probably wish they were not blessed with) in that richer groups in contemporary society do not take easily to living in close geographical proximity to them. The poor therefore exert a social pressure which can vary in its form from a mere felt presence, through a gross exhibition of all those social pathologies associated with poverty, to a fully fledged riot. The latter helps to open up the housing market to the poor most marvellously" (Harvey, 1973, pp. 172–3).

From mixed to segregated neighbourhoods

Intra-urban migration has been observed in a few studies, some of which show how housing segregation develops.

One such study was in Crawley (Heraud, 1968) where the development corporation housing (rented and subsidised) initially accommodated a considerable mix of social classes. But over time some of those tenants moved into owner-occupied houses, and the movers were of a higher social class than the average for development corporation tenants. The movers' dwellings were taken by people of a social class similar to that of the tenants remaining. As the owner-occupied houses were built in estates separate from the development corporation houses, those movements slowly produced neighbourhoods segregated by class.

Similar movements were found by Willmott (1963). He observed the emigration from Dagenham of middle-class residents—those who had been middle-class or aspiring middle-class when they moved there, those who had become middle-class while living there, and children with middle-class jobs and values and with working-class parents. Part of the reason for the emigration, Willmott suggests, is the uniformity of the housing in Dagenham: there was nothing bigger, of a better standard, or for sale. Hence Dagenham grew into a one-class town, social segregation on a huge scale.

INDEX TO REFERENCES IN CHAPTER 9

BARBOLET, R. H., 1969, *Housing Classes and the Socio-ecological System*, CES, UWP4, Centre for Environmental Studies, London.

BLAIR, T. L., 1969, "Social systems analysis", *Official Architecture and Planning*, vol. 32.

BURGESS, E. W., 1925, "The growth of the city", in Park, R. E. *et al.*, *The City*, The University of Chicago Press.

Dyos, H. J., 1961, *Victorian Suburb*, Leicester University Press.

Evans, A. W., 1973, *The Economics of Residential Location*, Macmillan, London.

Fisher, J. C., 1962, "Planning of the city of socialist man", *Journal of the American Institute of Planners*, vol. 28, no. 4.

Harvey, D., 1973, *Social Justice and the City*, Arnold, London.

Heraud, B. J., 1968, "Social class and the new towns", *Urban Studies*, vol. 5.

Hoyt, H., 1939, *The Structure and Growth of Residential Neighbourhoods in American Cities*, Federal Housing Administration, Washington.

Housing and Construction Statistics, 1974, no. 11, HMSO, London.

Kirwan, R. and Ball, M., 1973, "The micro-economic analysis of a local housing market", papers of the 1973 Urban Economics Conference, Centre for Environmental Studies, London.

Mann, P., 1965, *An Approach to Urban Sociology*, Routledge & Kegan Paul, London.

Murdie, R. A., 1971, "The social geography of the city", in Bourne, L. S. (ed.), *Internal Structure of the City*, OUP, New York.

Musil, J., 1968, "The development of Prague's ecological structure", in Pahl, R. E. (ed.), *Readings in Urban Sociology*, Pergamon, London.

Muth, R. F., 1969, *Cities and Housing*, Chicago University Press.

Pahl, R. E., 1965, *Urbs in rure*, LSE Geographical Paper no. 2. London.

Pahl, R. E., 1968 (a) *Readings in Urban Sociology*, Pergamon, London.

Pahl, R. E., 1968 (b) *Spatial Structure and Social Structure*, CES WP10, Centre for Environmental Studies, London.

Pahl, R. E., 1970, *Patterns of Urban Life*, Longmans, London.

Rex, J. A. and Moore, R., 1967, *Race, Community and Conflict*, OUP, London.

Rex, J. A., 1968, "The sociology of a zone of transition", in Pahl, R. E. (ed.), *Readings in Urban Sociology*, Pergamon, London.

Richardson, H. W., 1971, *Urban Economics*, Penguin, Harmondsworth.

Robson, B. J., 1969, *Urban Analysis: a Study of City Structure*, CUP, London.

Schelling, T. C., 1971, "On the ecology of micro-motives", *The Public Interest*, Fall issue.

Willmott, P., 1963, *The Evolution of a Community*, Routledge & Kegan Paul, London.

Wingo, L., 1961, *Transportation and Urban Land*, John Hopkins Press, Baltimore.

Watson, C. J., 1973, *Household Movement in West Central Scotland*, CURS, University of Birmingham.

FURTHER READING FOR CHAPTER 9

Berry, B. J. L. and Horton, F. E., 1970, *Geographic Perspectives on Urban Systems*, Prentice Hall, New Jersey, chapters 10, 11.

Bourne, L. S. (ed.), 1971, *Internal Structure of the City*, OUP, New York, parts III, V.

Carter, H., 1972, *The Study of Urban Geography*, Arnold, London, chapter 11.

Evans, A. W., 1973, *The Economics of Residential Location*, Macmillan, London.

Goodall, B., 1972, *The Economics of Urban Areas*, Pergamon, Oxford, chapter 6.

Hirsch, W. Z., 1973, *Urban Economic Analysis*, McGraw Hill, New York, chapter 3.

Jones, E., 1966, *Towns and Cities*, OUP, London, chapter 7.

LAMBERT, C. and WEIR, D. (eds.), 1975, *Cities in Modern Britain*, Fontana, Glasgow, chapters 4 and 5.

PAHL, R. E. (ed.), 1968, *Readings in Urban Sociology*, Pergamon, London.

ROBSON, B. J., 1969, *Urban Analysis: a Study of City Structure*, CUP, London.

PAHL, R. E., 1975, *Whose City?*, Penguin, Harmondsworth, part 2.

Social Geography, 1972, Open University Press, Bletchley (D281 III 9–12).

TIMMS, D. W. G., 1971, *The Urban Mosaic*, CUP.

CHAPTER 10

Interactions between Traffic and Land Use

INTRODUCTION

Our approach to studying the city we described in Chapter 1 as the study of persons interacting. For persons to interact they usually have to travel, and the following quotation expresses well the place of transport in our study of cities. "The metropolis is, in effect, a massive communications switchboard through which contacts are maintained between friends, buyers and sellers, servants and served, helpers and helped. Within that switchboard, the communications and transportation systems comprise the channels through which links between interacting partners are joined. The transportation system ... is the vital medium through which the interdependencies of complex urban societies get satisfied—through which societal integration is accomplished" (Webber, 1969, p. 14). It is personal interaction with which this chapter is concerned, the movement of people not the movements of goods.

Our interest in the traffic of personal interactions is in how it, in turn, interacts with the city. How is the traffic influenced by the form of the city? How is the city influenced by the traffic? Those are questions about what we shall call the interaction between traffic and land use, which we shall study by looking at two "actions" or relationships: traffic as a function of land use and the transport system, land use as a function of the transport system. Those two relationships are not reciprocal: the reason why we talk of an interaction will be explained later.

First it is necessary to define two terms carefully. In the context of traffic studies, *land use* means activities described by type, by location, and by intensity. So the land use of a city includes the fact that in one location is an office block producing local government services on an area of 0.1 ha, accommodating 200 persons, 40% of whom have access to a private car. And it includes the fact that in another location live 200 persons at a net density of 125 p.p.ha, in 60 households, the average annual income of which is £3000, and 50% of which have one car, 10% two or more cars, 40% no car. (Land use is called by Blunden (1971, p. 11) land use potential—"a measure of the scale of socio-economic activity that takes place on a given area of land".)

In this same context, the *transport system* of a town includes all the roads, the capacity of every link and every intersection, the maximum safe or legal speed on every link, all the public transport routes and the time, speed, and frequency of every service, private travel costs, public travel costs, the cost of time spent in travelling, car parking costs and possibilities, and so on.

So, when we say that traffic is a function of land use and the transport system we are saying: it is possible to *explain* traffic as the *effect* of land use and the transport system. If we know the theory which provides that explanation, and if we know the land use and the transport system of a particular town, we can predict the passenger movements on every link in the system, by trip purpose, mode of travel, origin and destination. Also, if land use or the transport system changes, we can predict how traffic will change (on the assumption that nothing else changes).

Similarly, when we say that land use is a function of the transport system we are saying: it is possible to *explain* land use as the *effect* of the transport system. That is, however, an ambitious claim which is difficult to test: the reason is that land use changes slowly, so the land use at any time is the effect of causes stretching back many years. So what is usually meant by the statement is: if the transport system of a town changes, land use also will change as a direct result. With the theory of that relationship it is possible to predict the changes in land use caused by the changes in the transport system (if nothing else changes).

Now we can explain the connection between the two relationships. The theory which explains traffic as a function of land use and the transport system has been developed in response to pressing practical questions of the following kind: if car ownership increases, how will traffic increase? If population growth is housed in new housing estates in given locations, what will be the effects on traffic? Then the questions follow: if traffic changes as predicted, will the present transport system be able to cope? If not, how should the transport system be changed? So the theory has been developed in order to predict the need for changes in the transport system and to test alternative proposals for such changes. However, whenever a transport system is changed we have to remember the second theory—that land use is a function of the transport system. So changing the transport system will cause land use to change. That will cause further changes in traffic, which may need further changes in the transport system.

For example, suppose that the public transport in a city region is running at a heavy loss. The Passenger Transport Executive is considering reducing the service, in order to save money. That possible change in the transport system is likely to cause changes in traffic—more people travel by cars, fewer people travel by bus and rail. Suppose that, even if that happened, there would be no more roads built. Then, congestion on the roads and buses leading to the city centres would increase—a further change in the transport system. As a result, employers, shopkeepers, restauranteurs, etc. might consider moving out of the centre, and shoppers and commuters would be less willing to visit the centre. The consequence would be decentralisation and suburbanisation (see Chapter 8)—a change in land use.

Alternatively, the predicted increase in car use caused by the proposed reduction in public transport might be met by a different response: the city council might improve the radial roads leading to the city centre. Then the centre would become more accessible to the housing areas by which the new roads passed, certain suburbs and commuter villages. These areas would become more attractive to city centre workers, so developers would build more housing there—a change in land use caused by a change in the transport system.

So there are various possible consequences of a decision to cut public transport, consequences for traffic, for the transport system, for land use. It is clear that theories are needed for predicting such consequences.

The connection between the two transport theories can be represented as:

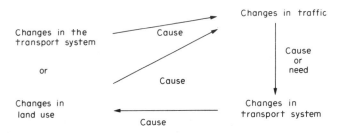

Changes in the transport system

or

Changes in land use

Cause

Cause

Changes in traffic

Cause or need

Changes in transport system

Cause

It is in that sense that there is interaction between traffic and land use.

That the interaction is well known makes it all the more surprising that it is ignored so frequently in transport planning: transport plans usually propose changes in the transport system without considering the changes which that might cause in land use. So Proudlove (1968) criticises a transport study, "The effect on land use of road capacity falling below demand is not considered, but is likely to lead to rapid changes which could invalidate the assumptions...". A similar criticism is made of the Buchanan Report by Beesley and Kain (1964). They point out that the Report made traffic forecasts for existing towns with their existing urban structures. But if those structures should change (e.g. as a spontaneous response to congestion or to traffic restraint), traffic forecasts would be different, and then transport proposals should be different. And Bruton says, "In the transport studies completed to date, changes in the location of activities (and ultimately land uses) in respect of the implementation of transport system proposals are not considered as part of the process (of transport planning)" (Bruton, 1974, p. 194).

One further point needs explaining in this introduction—why we refer throughout this chapter to traffic *theories* when it is customary to call them traffic *models*. The reason is as follows. There is an important distinction between models, which try to *simulate* processes, and theories, which try to *explain* processes (see Ryan, 1970, Chap. 4). Theories advance knowledge more than do models, so it is at theories not models that we should be aiming, and theories have to pass more rigorous tests than models. Hence we should not be content with models when we might have theories. As a result we should always put our hypotheses to the more searching tests appropriate to theories. (Sometimes the distinction between theories and models is made by distinguishing between predictive and descriptive models—see, for example, Bullock *et al.* 1972—and sometimes by distinguishing between analytic and descriptive models—see for example, Harris, 1968.)

THEORIES TO EXPLAIN TRAFFIC

"There is nothing as practical as a good theory" is particularly applicable to traffic: the practical need for theories to explain traffic is great. Before such theories were available, some traffic forecasts were made by projecting past trends, but the need is not so much for traffic *forecasts* as for traffic *predictions*—if that road is built, how much traffic will use it? If petrol doubles in price, how many people will transfer from cars to buses?

So theories are needed to explain traffic, and one of the first popular statements of the basis of current traffic theory appeared in *Traffic in Towns* (1963, p. 33). "Vehicles do not of course move about the roads for mysterious reasons of their own. They move only because people want them to move in connection with activities which they (the people) are engaged in. Traffic is therefore a function of activities. This is fundamental."

So the theory starts with *activities* located in *traffic zones*. Those activities in zones *generate* traffic: each zone both produces and attracts *trips* (e.g. a residential zone produces trips to work and attracts trips from work). The trips produced by a given zone are *distributed* between other zones, according to the trip purpose, the activities in the attracting zones, and the difficulties of travelling from the origin to the destination. Those trips between zones choose various transport *routes*, depending on network speeds, congestion, etc., a process known as *trip assignment*. And the people making the trips choose by what *modes* to travel—by car, bus, or train.

That theory of traffic is called the four-stage theory—generation, distribution, modal-split, and assignment. "The objective...is to

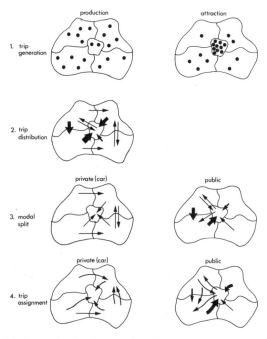

Fig. 10.1. Stages in the theory of traffic (by courtesy of John Wiley and Sons Ltd.).

predict the flows V_{rimp}, i.e. the volume of trips going from zone r to zone i by mode m and path p. In the four-step models, equilibrium calculations are structured into a sequence of four-steps; this amounts to estimating V_{rimp} in a series of successive approximations, first V_r, then V_{ri}, then V_{rim}, and finally V_{rimp}" (OECD Road Research Group, 1974, p. 23). The four stages are shown diagrammatically in Fig. 10.1 (after Wilson, 1974. Copyright © John Wiley and Sons

Ltd). Here we shall give a brief description of each stage. (The four-stage theory is the one most commonly used, but there are other theories. One—the demand/supply equilibrium model—will be mentioned below.)

Trip generation

The theory says that trip generation by a traffic zone depends on—the land uses and intensity of development in the zone, the social characteristics of the people performing the activities in the zone, the quality of the transport system in the study area. For example, a one hectare zone will generate more trips if it is used for industry than for housing, if the plot ratio is 2:1 rather than 1:1, if the workers have more cars, or if the zone is connected to a good transport system. The theory says also that which of those variables is important, and the relative weights of the important variables, depends on the trip purpose (e.g. the trips to work which a residential zone generates depend on the number of employed residents, a variable which has no effect on the trips to shop). Using that theory we can predict the trips produced by and attracted to every zone for every trip purpose (and hence we can produce tables such as Table 10.1).

One of the weaknesses of the four-stage theory should be mentioned here. It is that trip generation depends on the quality of the transport system, yet that quality is difficult to measure so is usually not included in the prediction. So the theory calibrated for one area

TABLE 10.1. HOME TO WORK TRIPS, PREDICTED BY TRIP GENERATION THEORY

		Zone of destination				Total trips produced
		A	B	C	D	
zone of origin	A	trip generation theory does not predict these entries in the matrix cells				MA
	B					MB
	C					MC
	D					MD
total trips attracted		NA	NB	NC	ND	

should be applied only to study areas with the same quality of transport system. Yet the theory might be used in a transport study which results in a change in the transport system which, therefore, causes a change in trip generation. When the man-in-the-street says, sceptically of road improvements: Traffic expands to fill the road space available, he is in effect criticising the trip generation theory for that weakness.

That mistake, and others, in the four-stage theory of traffic are avoided by the demand/supply equilibrium theory. People demand to use the transport system, and the size of their demand varies with the cost and convenience of making a trip. But that cost and convenience vary with the number of people using the transport system. If the cost of making a trip changes because of a better road, dearer parking, etc., then demand changes, which changes use, which changes the cost of making a trip (OECD Road Research Group, 1974).

Trip distribution

Trip distribution theories explain how the trips produced by one zone are distributed between the attracting zones, so they enable us to fill in the empty cells in Table 10.1 so as to produce tables such as Table 10.2. The trips from one zone to another are called "interzonal transfers".

TABLE 10.2. HOME TO WORK TRIPS, PREDICTED BY TRIP GENERATION AND TRIP DISTRIBUTION THEORIES

		Zone of destination (j)				Total trips produced
		A	B	C	D	
zone of origin (i)	A	—	TAB	TAC	TAD	$\Sigma_j T_{Aj} = MA$
	B	TBA	—	TBC	TBD	$\Sigma_j T_{Bj} = MB$
	C	TCA	TCB	—	TCD	$\Sigma_j T_{Cj} = MC$
	D	TDA	TDB	TDC	—	$\Sigma_j T_{Dj} = MD$
total trips attracted		$\Sigma_i T_{iA}$ = NA	$\Sigma_i T_{iB}$ = NB	$\Sigma_i T_{iC}$ = NC	$\Sigma_i T_{iD}$ = ND	

There are two trip distribution theories in common use by transport planners—the gravity theory and the opportunities theory. (Other methods are used—e.g. growth factor methods, multiple regression methods—but those are models and could never be considered as theories.) It would not be appropriate here to describe the theories in more than a few lines.

The gravity theory says that trips are distributed between destinations according to the attractions of the destinations and to the difficulty of travelling to the destinations. (Hence, the form of the theory is similar to the form of the spatial interaction theory for predicting how people choose which service centres to visit—see Chapter 7.) The opportunities theory says that the probability of a trip ending in a given zone can be predicted: multiplying that probability (P_j) by the total number of trips produced by a zone (M_i) gives the number of trips starting in i and ending in j (T_{ij}).

Modal split

Another property of traffic that we want to be able to explain is the modal split, the method of travel used for the trip. Is it by public transport (bus or train) or by private transport (car)? (The traffic theories described here do not try to explain traffic on foot or by bicycle.)

Some people, of course, have no choice of travel mode. Such are people without access to a car (e.g. members of a household with no car, children whose parents are unable or unwilling to act as chauffeurs), and people living in places where there is no public transport (usually rural areas well away from cities: in such places, the difficulties experienced by households without cars decreases the number of trips generated by such households—see earlier). So it is only some members of car-owning households in urban or urban fringe areas who have a choice of travel mode. How do they exercise that choice?

The theory says that the choice depends on three things—on the properties of the journey (e.g. the purpose of the journey: trips from home to school are more commonly by public transport than trips from home to shops), on the properties of the traveller (of which properties, access to a car is the *sine qua non* of being able to choose how to travel: of all car-owning households, it is found that the higher the socio-economic status of the household the less likely it is that public transport will be chosen), on the properties of the transport system (e.g. the relative travel time of the trip from door-to-door by public and by private transport, the relative travel cost, the relative level and convenience of service).

Trip assignment

In such ways, various theories try to explain the number, purpose, and mode of inter-zonal trips. Along what routes will those trips be made? To a large extent, public transport users have the routes of their trips chosen for them. But how do car-drivers choose their routes? Trip assignment theories try to answer that question by stating that people choose that route which gives the shortest travelling time.

The "minimum time path" from one zone to another can be calculated from a knowledge of the travel speed on each link of the network, when no other traffic is using that link. However, travel speed depends not only on the physical properties of a link and on legal maximum speeds, but also on the amount of traffic using the link: more traffic causes more congestion which reduces travel speed. So the assignment of trips to routes is not just a matter of calculating minimum time paths when there is no congestion (called the "all-or-nothing" assignment method). As more and more trips are assigned to a link, so congestion decreases travel speed on that link, so that route may cease to be the minimum time path. If so, traffic will use another route, thus changing travel speeds on the other links. (Fortunately, the complicated assignment procedure—the "capacity restraint" assignment method—can be done on a computer.)

Where a new motorway is added to an existing network, the theory that people choose the minimum time path does not predict well the amount of traffic which diverts on to the new motorway. So a theory of *traffic diversion* is used which states that, for all trips between one zone and another, the proportion diverting to the new motorway depends on the relative *travel resistance* of the old and the new routes.

Testing the theories

As we explained earlier, theories of traffic as a function of land use and the transport system have been developed to meet a practical need—the need to predict changes in traffic when the causal conditions change (e.g. if car ownership changes, if a new shopping centre is built). That practical situation has produced the following method of testing the theories.

The relevant properties of the existing land use and of the existing transport system are measured, and existing traffic flows are measured too. Some version of the traffic theory just described is chosen and applied to that existing situation, and calibrated so that with the values of existing land use and of the existing transport system, the theory predicts traffic flows as near as possible to existing observed traffic flows. (For examples of such testing of a trip generation theory and a trip distribution theory see *London Traffic Survey*, 1966, Vol. II, appends. J and R.)

In that way, the chosen traffic theory is tested afresh for every transport plan. However, that is not an ideal way of testing theory (not just traffic theory but any theory—see Distributive Trades EDC, 1970 and Harris, 1968), because predicted traffic flows are tested against the same observed traffic flows which were used to calibrate the theory. (Although that way of testing is not ideal it is nevertheless useful: if the theory were totally wrong, "goodness-of-fit" between predicted and observed values would always be bad.) The real test is after the land use or the transport system has changed: how do the observed traffic flows in that new situation compare with the traffic flows that were predicted for that new situation? Unfortunately, such rigorous testing is rarely applied to traffic theories. (For an exception see Aitken and White, 1972. In that case, the theory stood the test well.)

In the absence of such rigorous testing, how do we know whether the traffic theories outlined above are true? We must remain sceptical, and one thing in particular reinforces that scepticism. It is that the constants in the equations have to be calibrated afresh for each transport study. It is a serious weakness of the theories that that is so, for the aim is always to produce a *universal* theory, one that explains all situations of a given type. As Harris (1968) says, it should be possible to apply models and parameters developed for one city to another city. "... such a test imposes ... the responsibility for a general analytic framework which is transferable to very different situations and for the derivation of relatively invariant parameters" (p. 406).

TRANSPORT THEORIES TO EXPLAIN LAND USE

Many times in this book we have said that locational decisions are made for transport reasons. For example, in Chapter 7 we discussed central place theory and its claim that shops and offices locate by reference to the location of consumers: in Chapter 8 we said that manufacturing firms often cluster in order to enjoy external economies of scale, because if they were dispersed transport costs would be too high for such economies to be exploited: in Chapter 9 we referred to explanations of residential location in terms of journey-to-work costs. Our practical need is to be able to predict how known changes in the transport system will cause land use to change. Do any of the theories discussed so far enable us to do that? Are there any other theories which could help us?

It should be possible to use any transport theory of location to predict changes in location caused by changes in transport. An example will show how. For our example we shall take the Lowry model, as it is one of the few such theories which has been widely applied. (Lowry, 1964. For a simple description of the model and its modifications see Lee, 1973, Chap. 6.)

The Lowry model says (among other things) that residential location is influenced by employment location, and that the location of local services is influenced by the location of residences. We shall now describe the transport theories of location which lie behind those statements.

People decide where to live according to the location of jobs and the difficulties of travelling to those jobs. So employment in zone i attracts a certain number of people to live in zone j (P_{ij}) according to the amount of employment in i (E_i) and some measure of the difficulty of travelling between i and j ($f(d_{ij})$). That is, $P_{ij} = K_1 E_i f_1 (d_{ij})$ (K_1 is a constant). So the total population living in zone $j = P_j = K_1 \Sigma_i E_i f_1(d_{ij})$. Entrepreneurs decide where to provide their shops and other personal services by reference to where people live and to the difficulties of travelling from homes to local services. Then the total employment in local services in zone $j = S_j = K_2 \Sigma_i P_i f_2(d_{ij})$ where K_2 is a constant, P_i = population living in zone i, and $f_2(d_{ij})$ is a measure of the difficulty of travelling from zone i to zone j.

Those transport theories of location can be made operational by calculating empirically the values of K_1 and K_2 and the forms of the functions f_1 and f_2. With the theories in a usable form, Lowry used them to predict the locations of population and local services generated by a given amount of employment in given locations, with an unchanging transport system. He could have used the theories to predict changes in the locations of population and local services caused by given changes in the transport system, with an unchanging amount and location of employment: the changes in the transport system would have caused changes in the relative difficulties of travelling between zones, $f_1(d_{ij})$ and $f_2(d_{ij})$. One British application of the Lowry model (Cripps and Foot, 1970) uses it similarly to predict the effects on population caused by the introduction of new employment: the possibility of using it to predict the effects of changes in the transport system is discussed but not pursued. (Another transport theory of location which offers similar possibilities is the Hansen residential model, which tries to explain residential growth around a city in terms of accessibility to employment and the availability of vacant land. Changes in the transport system would affect the relative accessibilities of the vacant plots. For a discussion see Blunden, 1971, Chap. 6.)

The question must now be raised: why do transport planners not consider the likely effects on land use of their proposed changes to the transport system (see earlier) when there are so many transport theories of location (only one of which has been discussed above)? The answer is simple and regrettable: hardly any of the transport theories of location are in a form in which they can be used to make testable predictions. The Lowry model is one of the few exceptions, and that model does not try to answer all locational questions: moreover, we should not assume that the Lowry model gives correct answers. (Lowry, 1964, is quite open about the proportion of actual locations which his model cannot explain.) Another exception is a theory developed by Lathrop and Hamburg (1965), and they do use it to predict changes in land use caused by changes in transport. (For a discussion of location theories which are usable and which are being developed in the United States see Harris, 1968.)

In the absence of such theories, we turn to *impact studies*—studies of land use and the locations of activities before and after a major change in the transport system. However, we must not expect much enlightenment from impact studies made in a theoretical vacuum, for we need theories to direct our fact-collecting. Certainly, the one major impact study in Britain, a study of the effect of the new Severn Bridge on activities in South Wales and the South West, tells us little which would be generally applicable to other situations, except that the effects do not appear quickly (Cleary and Thomas, 1973).

Our ignorance remains. We do not know the consequences for land use of changes in the transport system. In this void, claims rush in to fill the vacuum, creating cold draughts which no student or planner of cities can ignore. Some examples, all important for urban planning, are given below.

It is claimed that changes in transport have so lowered the relative importance of transport costs in total production costs that for many manufacturing firms transport costs are irrelevant to the choice of location. (See Luttrell, 1964. See also the Toothill Report, 1961, which said, "In short, we found nothing in our enquiries to support the view that transport costs are a significant additional burden on manufacturing industry in industrial Scotland", para. 8.16.)

It is claimed that some interurban roads "open up" underdeveloped regions, bringing economic benefits of greater production and employment. (For a discussion of that claim see Gwilliam, 1970.) Hence investment in roads is a good instrument of regional development policy. (That claim is made in the Hunt Report, 1969.) The need for such a theory was felt in the study of the effect on North Wales of a new road across the Dee estuary. Would the new road allow firms from Merseyside to move in to North Wales, or firms from North Wales to move into Merseyside? In the end, a guess had to be made: that the new road crossing would allow people who worked in Merseyside to live in North Wales, and that it would have no effect on industry ("Deeside Planning Study", 1970, p. 50).

The motor car, it is often said, is the "solvent of urban form", dissolving locational ties (e.g. allowing people who work in the city to live in the city's rural hinterland—see Chapter 4).

It is observed that warehouses are moving out of their city-centre locations. The reason, it is suggested, is that congestion in the cities and improved roads outside the cities have shifted the location of maximum accessibility to suppliers and to customers (see Chapter 8).

For many cities, proposals are being made to reduce the number of work journeys into the city centre which are made by car (e.g. using parking schemes, subsidised public transport, road pricing). Yet the effect of those proposals on the location of firms now in the centre and on the rate of movement of firms out of the centre seems not to have been considered (see, for example, West Midlands Regional Study, 1971).

It is disturbing that the study of the interaction between traffic and land use is so imbalanced: theories of traffic are so well developed and transport theories of land use are so badly developed.

INDEX TO REFERENCES IN CHAPTER 10

AITKEN, J. M. and WHITE, R., 1972, "A comparison between traffic forecast and reality", *Traffic Engineering and Control*, vol. 14, no. 4.

BEESLEY, M. E. and KAIN, J. F., 1964, "Urban form, car ownership, and public policy", *Urban Studies*, vol. 1, no. 2.

BLUNDEN, W. R., 1971, *The Land-Use/Transport System*, Pergamon, Oxford.
BRUTON, M. J., 1974, "Transport planning", in Bruton, M. J. (ed.), *The Spirit and Purpose of Planning*, Hutchinson, London.
BULLOCK, N. *et al*, 1972, "The use of models in planning and the architectural design process", in Martin, L. and Marsh, L. (eds.), *Urban Space and Structures*, CUP.
CLEARY, E. J. and THOMAS, R. E., 1973, *The Economic Consequences of the Severn Bridge and its Associated Motorways*, Bath University Press.
CRIPPS, E. L. and FOOT, D. H. S., 1970, "The urbanisation effects of a third London airport", *Environment and Planning*, vol. 2, no. 2.
Deeside Planning Study, 1970, Shankland, Cox & Associates, London.
Distributive Trades EDC, 1970, *Urban Models in Shopping Studies*, HMSO, London.
GWILLIAM, K. M., 1970, "The indirect effects of highway development", *Regional Studies*, vol. 4, no. 2.
HARRIS, B., 1968, "Quantitative models of urban development", in Perloff, H. S. and Wingo, L. (eds.), *Issues in Urban Economics*, Johns Hopkins Press, Baltimore.
Hunt Report, 1969, *The Intermediate Areas*, Cmnd 3998, HMSO, London.
LATHROP, G. T. and HAMBURG, J. R., 1965, "An opportunity-accessibility model for allocating regional growth", *Journal of the American Institute of Planners*, vol. 31, no. 2.
LEE, C., 1973, *Models in Planning*, Pergamon, Oxford.
London Traffic Survey, 1966, Greater London Council.
LOWRY, I. S., 1964, *A Model of Metropolis*, The Rand Corporation, Santa Monica.
LUTTRELL, W. F., 1964, "Industrial location and employment policy", *Proceedings of the Town and Country Planning School*, Town Planning Institute, London.
OECD Road Research Group, 1974, *Urban Traffic Models: Possibilities for Simplification*, OECD, Paris.
PROUDLOVE, J. A., 1968, "Some comments on West Midlands Transport Study", *Traffic Engineering and Control*, vol. 10, no. 7.
RYAN, A., 1970, *The Philosophy of the Social Sciences*, Macmillan, London.
Toothill Report, 1961, *Inquiry into the Scottish Economy*, Scottish Council, Edinburgh.
Traffic in Towns, 1963, HMSO, London.
WEBBER, M. M., 1969, *On Strategies for Transport Planning*, OECD, Paris.
West Midlands Regional Study, 1971, *A Developing Strategy for the West Midlands*, Birmingham.
WILSON, A. G., 1974, *Urban and Regional Models in Geography and Planning*, John Wiley, London.

FURTHER READING FOR CHAPTER 10

BERRY, B. J. L. and HORTON, F. E., 1970, *Geographic Perspectives on Urban Systems*, Prentice Hall, New Jersey, chapter 13.
BLUNDEN, W. R., 1971, *The Land-Use/Transport System*, Pergamon, Oxford.
BRUTON, M. J., 1974, *Introduction to Transportation Planning*, Hutchinson, London, 2nd ed.
HIRSCH, W. Z., 1973, *Urban Economic Analysis*, McGraw Hill, New York, chapter 4.
KRUEKEBERG, D. A. and SILVER, A. L., 1974, *Urban Planning Analysis*, John Wiley, New York, chapter 10.

LEIBBRAND, K., 1970, *Transportation and Town Planning*, Leonard Hill, London, parts A, B, and C.

MEYER, J. R., KAIN, J. F., WOHL, M., 1965, *The Urban Transportation Problem*, Harvard University Press, part I.

Traffic in Towns, 1963, HMSO, London (The Buchanan Report).

CHAPTER 11

The Effects of Public Policies on Cities

INTRODUCTION

We are asking the question: how do cities work? and our answer so far has been: by the interactions of private persons, households, and firms, making decisions and carrying them out with the *private market powers* available to them—e.g. choosing where to shop, where to build shops, which route to take, how many workers to employ.

The possibility of private bodies using *public governmental* powers either formally (e.g. as electors or councillors) or informally (e.g. as pressure groups or by corruptly using public powers) has so far been ignored. And given little attention so far have been the actions of public bodies (in particular the local authority) using governmental powers in order deliberately to affect the ways that cities work.

We can no longer avoid that subject. No British city (and probably few cities anywhere) is left to work "on its own": we have mentioned already the imposition of green belts (Chapter 3), land use zoning (Chapter 8), restrictions on industrial building and encouragement of industrial movement (Chapter 6). Moreover, it is probably true that no city could work "on its own": there are some provisions and regulations which cannot be made adequately by private market powers but which are essential if the private market is to continue to operate in and to shape cities, such as housing for poor people, or a police force. In that way, the city would be similar to a market economy which, as the Great Depression showed, may collapse without government regulation and intervention.

So we cannot understand how cities work without knowing:
why cities are not left to work on their own;
the instruments for public intervention in the interactions between
   private persons and organisations;
how the instruments are used for public policy;
the effects of public policy on the ways that cities work.

Those are questions about governmental power being used so that urban processes are the outcome not only of market decisions but also of political decisions. So they are questions of *public policy* in cities (using Dearlove's definition of public policy as "a pattern of resources committed by government which has an effect on those outside government". Dearlove, 1973, p. 2). The subject is huge, and we can do no more than give a brief introduction.

METHODS OF ANALYSIS

Our subject is important, but how do we approach it? How can we study the effects of public policy on the city? We can give two general answers.

We can start by studying private persons and organisations interacting, then study the effects of public intervention on that system of private interactions. That method we might call the *behavioural* approach, because it starts with the behaviour of private bodies within a given social situation. Alternatively, we can start with the system of rules (laws, conventions, organisations, expectations, definitions, etc.) which constrain the interactions of private bodies. What are those rules, what determines them, how do people act within them? That might be called the *structural* approach, because it starts with the institutions which structure and regulate private actions.

So far in this book (it is easy to see) we have taken an approach (systems, ecological, individualistic—Chapter 1) consistent with the behavioural method: Chapters 3–10 have been about private interactions in an urban world largely free of government intervention, we have used explicitly the economic method of supply and demand, we have stressed that before planners act they should understand how the private market works, and even the title of this chapter indicates the behavioural approach. That does not mean, however, that we reject the structural approach: the study of public policy should use either or both of the approaches as appropriate. And what is appropriate for the purpose of this book is the behavioural approach. There are three reasons.

The structural approach tries to explain how power is distributed in cities. Pahl (1975) suggests four different explanations:

The 'pure' managerialist model	control by the professional officers of the local government of the city;
The statist model	control by national government;
The control by capitalists model	control by private capitalists, or by others in the interests of the private capitalists;
The pluralist model	control by the above three groups in permanent tension with each other, also, by the dominant political party. (I would add, too the market power held by the non-élite.)

Which explanation is truest for British cities is not yet agreed: partly the answer which is taken for truth will depend on empirical testing, partly it will depend on the ideology of the answerer. The answer which I give provisionally is a pluralist explanation. If power is distributed that way, private persons and organisations have a lot more freedom of choice than with power centralised in some elite. The behavioural approach can explain more in cities where power is dispersed than where power is centralised. So by applying the behavioural approach to a pluralist model we are not preventing ourselves from giving useful answers to the question: how do cities work?

The second reason for concentrating on this approach is that many people want to understand how cities work in order to change and improve them. It is unlikely (in my opinion) that British cities will be changed by a deliberate restructuring of the distribution of power in society. If that is true it follows that most changes to British cities will be marginal, interventions in the systems by which they work at present (e.g. reforming housing finance, planning restrictions on hypermarkets). So the urban reformer needs knowledge of how cities work at present. That we have tried to state in Chapters 3–10, describing not the power context, the structure, but how private bodies act within that context. If planned changes to cities were to be more radical, the activist would need more knowledge than can be found by the behavioural approach, knowledge of alternative power contexts and of how private bodies would act in different contexts.

The third reason for concentrating here on the behavioural approach is, quite simply, that it is easier than the structural approach. The latter takes us deeper under the surface of society. It is an exciting journey, but difficult and often frustrating: for this book we do not need to make it, so we may stay at home in comfort. (For structural approaches to the study of cities see Harvey, 1973, and Bailey, 1975.)

There is another methodological question before we can start on substantive issues. This book aims to describe how cities *do* work, not how they *should* work. So this chapter will describe how public policy is used, not how it should be used. However, these two topics are connected (although the positive and normative questions are locally separate), because government intervenes in order to change the ways that cities work (see later). Therefore, the ways that public policy *does* work are partly the result of the actions of people implementing the ways that they think public policy *should* work. So our description of the actual working of public policy will be affected by ideas of how it ought to work.

WHY IS THERE PUBLIC INTERVENTION IN CITIES?

"Governmental, or public, action is a response to (or an attempt to cure) what are seen as public problems" (Dearlove, 1973, p. 211). That is the view that cities are not left to work "on their own", that the system of private interactions is regulated publicly, because such a private market system produces results which are considered to be unsatisfactory. If enough people with enough influence hold that opinion, then laws are passed and implemented so that the private market system is modified to produce better results. The politicians in power might want to change it for the better, or they might want to stop it from changing for the worse.

That view of public intervention is so important that we shall use it shortly—but not until it has been challenged. First, it does not stand as an explanation of political power throughout British history. Kings and barons wielded power because they could, because they believed they had a right to, and because the people allowed them to. Any laws reflected that situation. With the growth of individualism and the change in economic integration from redistribution to market exchange (Harvey, 1973, chap. 6), the exercise of political power required a different legitimation: private persons and organisations should be left to get on with their own business and political intervention needs to be justified. The liberal political economists of the 19th century expressed that attitude definitively: for example, Mill, for his day a defender of government enterprise, has in his *Principles of Political Economy* (1900) the last chapter "Of the grounds and limits of the *laissez-faire* or non-interference principle". We are concerned to explain public intervention in these present conditions only.

Second, there is the contradictory view that government is about gaining and keeping advantages, advantages of wealth, power, or status. They might be personal advantages (e.g. politicians corruptly using governmental powers) or group advantages (e.g. the wealthy trying to maintain an economic system which favours them and fighting off attempts by the poor to create a system in their favour, or property interests controlling a city government and using it for their benefit). The classic story of the fight over public housing in Chicago in the late 1940's (Meyerson and Banfield, 1955) is largely about politicians trying to maintain their party machines.

The trouble with that cynical, self-interest or group-interest view of public intervention in cities is that it is extremely difficult to test empirically: is it true or false? For example, studies of the motivations of local councillors do not support the simple self-interest view. Jones (1969), after a careful study of local government in Wolverhampton between 1888 and 1964, concludes "What is certain is that men do not become councillors simply to promote their own advantage or that of their economic group, nor do they leave the council when they fail to achieve these objectives" (p. 287). And, summarising several such studies, Bochel and Denver (1973) find a complex situation. "Whilst it is probably true that large numbers of people do enter city politics out of a real desire to serve the community, it is also true that later, some also see the chances to better themselves in business and politics, and even more come to enjoy the status, prestige, and power that being a councillor incurs" (p. 26). But is it not naive to expect politicians to give themselves away in answers about what moves them? Moreover, the powerful may not understand their own motives: they practise class interests unknowingly and innocently, while sincerely professing public interest because of their false consciousness: "patriotic noble-mindedness fights indignantly against such an unprincipled conception" (Engels).

So study the actions of politicians, not what they say! If, however, you fail to find any evidence of the already powerful using governmental power to their own advantage, that is because one of their powers is the ability to manipulate the issues that arise (so as to sustain their position) and publicity (so as to conceal their presence— Bochel and Denver, 1973). Alternatively, if the record of legislation and the uses made of it can be explained better by the public-interest than by the self-interest theory (as is so, I would argue, with the record of urban public policy in Britain over the last 100 years—public health, housing, highways, parks, land use, public transport, etc.), then neither does that refute the cynical view of public intervention. For such intervention can be interpreted as a record of minor concessions to change, no more than was necessary to preserve the power system and to delay the "crisis of capitalism", or some such. The self-interest theory takes us nowhere as long as it can be forever adapted so as to avoid refutation.

(One exception is when the self-interest is announced, when a pressure group openly and unashamedly enters politics in order to resist a particular change which would hurt its members, on the grounds: it is not fair that we alone should suffer. Such explicitly self-interested political action—e.g. opposition to the siting of a new prison, "don't clobber the motorist"—is not common in Britain.)

We can use the insights of the self-interest or group interest theory and avoid its disadvantages (as described above) by a modification of the public-interest theory. The statement, "Governmental, or public, action is a response to (or an attempt to cure) what are seen to be urban problems" (Dearlove, see above) must be supplemented with "and politicians see public problems selectively, often in a way which sustains the politicians' positions". So Dearlove continues, "there are no objective criteria as to what constitutes a public problem, and in any community there are likely to be differing views, for a problem will be defined as "public" to the extent that it is believed that the causes of that problem lie outside the control of individuals who are, by themselves, seen as incapable of providing a solution" (Dearlove, 1973, pp. 211, 212).

That raises the questions: why do different politicians hold different views of the public interest? and, from where do politicians get their views? Those are interesting and important questions, but structural questions so we shall ignore them here. However, we must be clear that those questions do not answer the further question: what is the *correct* view of the public interest? That is partly a moral question, as is made clear by the statement of the Reverend Robert Dale in 1884. "The gracious words of Christ, 'Inasmuch as ye did it unto one of these my brethren, even these least, ye did it unto me' will be addressed not only to those who with their own hands fed the hungry, and clothed the naked, and cared for the sick, but to those who supported a municipal policy which lessened the miseries of the wretched and added brightness to the life of the desolate" (quoted in Briggs, p. 201).

Using the modified public-interest view of public intervention in cities we can take a lead from Keynes ("soon or late it is ideas, not vested interests, which are dangerous"—i.e. potent—"for good or evil" Keynes, 1936, p. 384) and look for *ideas*. What are the ideas which lead to public intervention?

First, there are ideas of ethical standards: it is a bad thing that people should live next to dirty, noisy factories; it is a bad thing that people cannot travel easily around a city; it is a bad thing that time and resources should be wasted in traffic jams; it is a bad thing that people are killed and injured in road accidents; it is a bad thing that people are unemployed or have no choice of work. If the reality of urban life falls short of these standards, then people say; something should be done!

The second set of ideas is why such public problems exist. Some of the problems arise because persons act individually, knowing that the sum of their individual actions will be undesirable, but unable individually to co-ordinate themselves so that the sum is desirable. Schelling (1971) examines what he calls "the ecology of micromotives", and gives examples of people spreading noise and dirt, knowing that if they alone did not, the improvement would be infinitesimal and knowing that if everybody did not, the improvement would be great. But how can personal morality be made a public asset?

Other public problems arise, many of them similar to those above, when certain conditions ("market imperfections" in economic jargon) apply and when production is in private hands. There might be external effects, when one firm affects others and that effect is unrequested and unpriced (e.g. pollution, congestion): there might be public goods which, once produced, are freely available to everyone and which therefore cannot be sold (e.g. street lighting, police protection) and impure public goods which provide a free service more conveniently for some than others (e.g. the location of a public facility); there might be a monopoly of supply causing low wages; there might be different rates of adjustment to change (e.g. to the suburbanisation of industry—Chapter 8—richer people have been able to respond more quickly than poorer people).

A different set of public problems arises because some people do things which (according to others) are not in their own interests. For example, people might be ignorant and shortsighted (about, for example, how to remain healthy or how to train for a job); they might choose to consume, if given the choice, too little of what are called "merit goods" (e.g. housing, education, health); they might be personally inadequate (e.g. carelessness causing road accidents, laziness causing low incomes).

Yet more public problems can arise if one group (e.g. landowners, the press, an industrialist) has and abuses excessive power. That can delay or exploit building redevelopment, restrict the choice of jobs available, raise the price of goods or housing, and so on.

We shall not continue describing the public problems and their causes, to tackle which governments intervene in cities. "In attempting to enumerate the necessary functions of government, we find them to be considerably more multifarious than most people are at first aware of, and not capable of being circumscribed by those very definite lines of demarcation which, in the inconsiderateness of popular discussion, it is often attempted to draw round them" (Mill, 1900, p. 480.)

Third, there are ideas about whether public intervention could alleviate the problems. If the cause of a problem is lack of coordination, or external effects, or public goods, it is easy to see how government could act to improve matters. "The government is not only an ultimate authority, when compulsion or exclusiveness is required, it is also an instrument for initiative on a large or monopolistic scale and it is the address to which people send their complaints when they do not like the way their environment is shaping up" (Schelling, 1971). At the other extreme, if the cause is personal inadequacy, choosing a public policy is much more difficult. There might be some urban problems which, although of public concern, politicians decide cannot be tackled.

Different people have different ideas on such matters, and it must be emphasised that the ideas which lead to public policy are those held by the people with the power to put them into action. For example, changes in the political composition of local councils have led to changes in transport planning policies (e.g. Nottingham and Worcester around 1973) when the new councillors had different ideas about social values (e.g. equality of opportunity to travel, curbing individual freedoms) than the old. And it is said that a modern physical environment is a town planner's value foisted on the working class because the town planners have the power (Davies, 1972).

WHAT ARE THE INSTRUMENTS OF PUBLIC INTERVENTION?

The instruments may be put into three categories—laws, financial arrangements, and organisations. In Britain, the laws are Acts of Parliament, often supplemented by central government circulars. The laws give the powers to set up public bodies, and then give the public bodies the powers to act: examples of the latter are the education Acts, the housing Acts, the town and country planning Acts. Such laws are central to public intervention, for the public corporations are subject to the doctrine of *ultra vires*: unlike private persons, who may do whatever they like unless expressly forbidden, public organisations can do nothing whatever unless expressly allowed.

The financial arrangements give the money and resources to the public bodies without which the legal powers could not be used. Examples are central grants for local transport and public housing, powers to levy rates locally, the rate support grant from central government, charges for the use of water, parking spaces, public housing.

And it is through the organisations—local authorities, regional health authorities, water boards, etc.—that public policy is made and implemented.

It would be inappropriate in this book to give even a general description of the laws and financial arrangements which support public policy in British cities. It would, however, be helpful to say a little about the organisations.

The organisations work at the national, regional and local levels: that body responsible at the city level (local government) is not the only public body which intervenes in the city processes. Central government sets the legal and financial framework within which local government and *ad hoc* local or regional bodies work: and also central government may intervene locally independently of the local government (e.g. the local policies of the Department of Health and Social Security, the Department of Industry, the Home Office).

The relationships between those public bodies are complex and difficult to understand. For example, although local government exists by the grace of central government and receives a high proportion of its income therefrom, nevertheless local governments have considerable freedom and exhibit a wide variety of actions (Dearlove, 1973; Boaden, 1971; Meacher, 1971). The Department of the Environment (central) has responsibility for local government and also for the physical environment: it can exercise the latter responsibility nationally but has no formal control over the other central departments which affect local issues and hence affect the former responsibility. Local government can use its experience of urban problems to persuade central government to change relevant laws or financial arrangements (e.g. for housing see Harloe *et al.*, 1973).

The organisations of central government (the House of Commons, M.P.s, civil servants, etc.) are better known than those of local government: also, local government has the more direct responsibility for public policy in cities: so the organisations of local government only will be outlined here (for a fuller description see Bochel and Denver, 1973).

Those organisations stipulated by Acts of Parliament are called statutory. There are local authorities, and there are *ad hoc* bodies such as regional health authorities, water boards, regional economic planning councils, and standing conferences of local authorities. The local authorities in England and Wales are organised in a two-tier system: the higher tier are counties, the lower are districts (Greater London is different). Each tier of local government has specific functions, and in the conurbations (where government is by *metropolitan* counties and *metropolitan* districts) the division of functions is slightly different than elsewhere. The policy-making body of the local authority is the Council, which delegates much of its power (but not its ultimate responsibility) to committees. Councillors are elected to the Council by the electoral system (e.g. in metropolitan areas, each electoral ward returns three councillors to the district and one to the county). Anyone may stand for election as a councillor (but not, unless adopted as such, as an official party candidate) and there is no deposit to be made or forfeited. The councillors appoint one of their members to be mayor for a year, who is chairman of council meetings but plays a largely ceremonial role as Chief Citizen. And last but not least is a vast army of council officials, not elected but employed by the council as professional advisors, administrators, teachers, bus drivers, and so on.

It is most important that we do not assume that those different parts of the local authority all work together, co-operating to implement agreed policies. We know that there is often conflict between councillors. Less well known are the conflicts between councillors and officers in different departments. The local authority is not a homogeneous organisation which decides and acts as if with one mind. (Some important implications of that are discussed later.)

As well as the statutory organisations are non-statutory ones. Political parties are perhaps the most important: most councillors in

Britain are associated with political parties and are chosen and supported by the local branch of a national party: and most elections are contested on party lines. Pressure groups are another type of non-statutory organisation—Chambers of Commerce, civic societies, trades unions representing council workers, community action groups, etc. The local press also often tries to be involved in local politics, urging one policy rather than another.

HOW THE INSTRUMENTS ARE USED

Those instruments are used for making, implementing, and maintaining public policy in cities. How are they used? How may the resulting policies be explained?

Three of the main theories are as follows: that councillors carry out the wishes of their electors; that councillors allow themselves to be used by pressure groups; and that public policy can be explained in terms of the socio-economic environment of the local government (e.g. the *per capita* income of the residents, the level of industrialisation). Dearlove shows that each of those theories is inadequate on its own, that even when combined they are still inadequate, for none includes the wills of the politicians making the policy: "...(the theories) deny that government assumes an autonomous or major role in the process" (Dearlove, 1973, p. 72). Boaden (1971) constructs and tests a theory which tries to explain public policy in terms of the local council as well as its environment (e.g. trying to explain spending on education in terms of the political composition of the council, the age and class structure of the population, rate resources, etc.). Apart from that, however, there is little we can say on the general theory of how instruments of public policy are used in cities.

In that void, we could write a list of the legislation which imposes duties on local authorities and other public bodies (e.g. to provide a police force, to supply pure water, to provide education for 5–16 year olds) or a list of the functions of local authorities (e.g. in metropolitan areas, districts have responsibility for education and social services whereas in non-metropolitan areas those two functions are the responsibility of the counties). But such lists would not do justice to, and would certainly not explain, the variety of policies between local authorities.

Another way of trying to fill the void is with case studies of urban public policy, e.g. the Brighton Marina ("A local government system", 1973), housing in Lambeth (Harloe *et al.*, 1973), housing renewal in Newcastle (Davies, 1972). But such case studies, while suggesting ways in which our general knowledge could be extended, do not take us along those ways.

So, instead of generalising or particularising about urban policy-making, we shall describe a general *method* which may be applied to investigating that in particular cases. It is a method which assumes that politicians and public officials are rational, and that they try to use some form of rational policy-making method (this is the "zero method" of Popper, 1961). We do not need to assume that they act thus self-consciously or even successfully—only that we can use a model of rationality for understanding and explaining the actions of people in public positions. The alternative assumption is that such people act willfully, or whimsically, or out of pique or caprice—i.e. irrationally, without using reason.

Our simple model of rationality can be represented in two parts. The first part describes the whole process of policy-making, and assumes that politicians and officers act rationally in what they see as the public interest.

(a) A problem is perceived
    (This depends on the ideology of the actors, their information, their constitutional and legislative duties, as well as on the condition of the urban society, its physical state, etc.)
(b) Alternative solutions to the problem are suggested
(c) Criteria for choosing the best solution are specified
    (These two stages depend on the disposition of the politicians and officers, the economic resources of local government, the legal and administrative possibilities, the knowledge and creativity of politicians and their advisers, etc.)
(d) The solutions are evaluated against the criteria, and the best solution is chosen.

The second part of the model of rationality describes stage (b) of the process, that stage when the question is asked: what means (solution) can we use to tackle the end (problem)? What will be the consequences of choosing this policy or that policy?

(a) Powers, used to implement
(b) public policy, which acts on
(c) instrumental variables, which act on
(d) any number of intermediate variables, which act on
(e) the policy variable, to achieve
(f) the policy end

These relationships are described by the theories of how cities work

(after Lipsey, 1966, p. 837).

So when it is proposed to create a more attractive environment to halt the flight of the middle classes from the city, or to build more roads to ensure the prosperity of the city's central area (both examples from City of Birmingham Structure Plan, 1973) we assume that some deliberate attempt has been made (however badly) to choose a policy purposefully with reference to its effects.

Our "zero method" of assuming rationality says that politicians and public officials employ some such rational model (for a much fuller model, see, for example Faludi, 1973, especially part III) when deciding how to use the available institutions for changing cities.

However, that method cannot tell us the whole story. It tries to tell us how individuals in public positions choose, within an institutional situation as they see it, policies and actions. Yet a public organisation, in particular a big local authority, is a complex institution containing many conflicts, and the decisions and actions that come out of it may not be what some of its members desired, may even be what none of its members desired. Meyerson and Banfield (1955) use a striking analogy. "The process by which a housing program for Chicago was formulated resembled somewhat the parlor game in which each player adds a word to a sentence which is passed around the circle of players: the player acts *as if* the words that are handed to him express some intention (i.e. as if the sentence that comes to him were *planned*) and he does his best to sustain the illusion. In playing this game the staff of the Authority was bound by the previous moves. ...It was up to the staff to finish the sentence in a way that would seem to be rational but this may have been an impossibility" (p. 269). Muchnick (1970) and Norman (1971) give examples of urban renewal in Britain where planning principles have not been dominant because other local authority departments have disagreed with the planning departments and won their points. Norman points out that "...the demolition and restructuring of the inner city...may be secured in a piecemeal fashion by the joint activities of the public health inspector, the architect, and the housing manager acting largely independently of the planner. The phasing and location of demolition and of subsequent land acquisition may reflect the public health inspector's principle of 'worst first' rather than the planner's timetable of phased redevelopment. The nature of redevelopment on a cleared site is likely to be dominated by the housing manager's interpretation of current housing requirements and the inadequacies of the housing stock rather than the planner's principle of 'social balance'."

If the current attempts in British local government to introduce corporate planning and programme—planning—budgeting systems are successful, the different parts of a local authority may work in a much more concerted way. We should not be too hopeful for that, however: Rapoport (1974) describes "systemic theories of conflict" which state that large systems often produce outcomes which are independent of the wishes of their members.

Certainly under present conditions, the ways in which persons in a public authority try to make and implement decisions can tell us only part of the story about how the instruments of public policy are used. The other part of the story is told by the institutions in which those persons work and through which their decisions are modified. We have some case studies of how policy decisions were made and implemented (e.g. Dennis, 1972, tells of the choice and administration of a housing plan in part of Sunderland) and politicians sometimes publish their revealing diaries (e.g. see the accounts by the erstwhile Minister of Housing and Local Government of why he permitted the overspill development at Chelmsley Wood and how he designated Central Lancashire New Town: Crossman, 1975). We have, however, little systematic knowledge about the effects of public institutions on public policy. The full story about how the instruments of public policy are used is very complex: "public policy analysis", as it is called, is a difficult study.

THE EFFECTS OF PUBLIC POLICY

We can use the second part of the model of rationality for analysing the connections between public policy and its effects on the city. We would expect, from our theories of how cities work, policy A to have effect B. Did it? we ask, and we try to answer with empirical studies.

If we find that the actual effects of a policy are different from those desired by the politicians and public officials, there may be three reasons why. One is that the actors used incorrect or inadequate theories (e.g. the 1947 nationalisation of development rights in land decreasing the supply of land, the 1972 Housing Finance Act driving up the price of private housing, see other examples from Chapter 2). Another is that the actors used incorrect facts (e.g. trying to stop the "drift to the south" of people when it had already ended). A third reason is that the outcome of several persons' individual decisions, combined and modified by the institution in which they work, was different from what any of the persons desired.

One complication which we (and the policy makers and officials) need to include in the theory of the relationships between means and ends is that the existence and use of public powers may modify the structure of the private system: it may not be just that private interests allow themselves to be manipulated by public policies, but that private interests learn of the public powers and adapt their actions accordingly. For example, commercial development in London since 1945 can only be understood as a response by property developers looking for loopholes in planning legislation (Marriott, 1969), and private landlords have changed their properties from unfurnished to furnished in order to avoid their tenants having security of tenure.

Can we say anything more general about the effects of public policy on how cities work? Have public policies been successful or unsuccessful? That is not an unreasonable question when you remember that local authorities employ 11% of the working population (and some of the 8% of the working population employed by central government also are working on urban public policy) (in the United Kingdom in 1973, see Central Statistical Office, 1974) and that local government accounts for 12% of total domestic expenditure (in the United Kingdom in 1973, current expenditure on goods and services and gross domestic fixed capital formation, see Central Statistical Office, 1974).

Obviously, this is not the place for a review of all that governmental activity. Instead we shall just state, with a few examples, the three possibilities. One is success. There is no doubt that government has succeeded in reducing some problems in urban areas: our streets are lit and swept, epidemics no longer sweep through the poorer areas of our cities, we enjoy parks and open spaces, the poorest do not always have the worst housing. Another possibility is failure, and exacerbating the problems. Perhaps some of the road building has reduced mobility overall by contributing to the deterioration of public transport: urban renewal has often reduced job and housing opportunities (see Chapter 2). The third possibility is failure, and no significant effect. For example, Hall concludes that the town and country planning activity since 1947 has had little effect on the process of suburbanisation, although the planning aim has usually been at self-contained and balanced communities (Hall *et al.*, 1973).

INDEX TO REFERENCES IN CHAPTER 11

BAILEY, J., 1975, *Social Theory for Planning*, Routledge & Kegan Paul, London.
A Local Government System, 1973, Open University Press, Bletchley (T241, 7–8).
BOADEN, N., 1971, *Urban Policy-Making*, CUP.
BOCHEL, J. M. and DENVER, D. T., 1973, "Politics in the city", in *The System of Control*, Open University Press (DT 201 19–21), Milton Keynes.
BRIGGS, A., 1968, *Victorian Cities*, Penguin, Harmondsworth.
Central Statistical Office, 1974, *National Income and Expenditure 1963–73*, HMSO, London.
City of Birmingham Structure Plan, 1973, *Report on the Options*, Birmingham.
CROSSMAN, R. H. S., 1975, *The Diaries of a Cabinet Minister*, Hamilton Cape, London.
DAVIES, J. G., 1972, *The Evangelistic Bureaucrat*, Tavistock Publications, London.
DEARLOVE, J., 1973, *The Politics of Policy in Local Government*, CUP.
DENNIS, N., 1972, *Public Participation and Planners' Blight*, Faber & Faber, London.
Department of Employment, 1973, *British Labour Statistics Yearbook 1971*, HMSO, London.
ENGELS, F., 1859, "Karl Marx: a contribution to the critique of political economy", in *Marx and Engels: Selected Works*, 1962, Lawrence & Wishart, London.
FALUDI, A., 1973, *Planning Theory*, Pergamon, Oxford.
HALL, P. *et al.*, 1973, *The Containment of Urban England*, PEP and Allen & Unwin, London.

HARLOE, M., ISSACHAROFF, R., and MINNS, R., "The organisational context of housing policy in inner London", in Donnison, D. and Eversley, D. (eds.), 1973, *London: Urban Patterns, Problems and Policies*, Heinemann, London.

HARVEY, D., 1973, *Social Justice and the City*, Arnold, London.

JONES, G. W., 1969, *Borough Politics*, Macmillan, London.

KEYNES, J. M., 1936, *The General Theory of Employment, Interest, and Money*, Macmillan, London.

LIPSEY, R. G., 1966, *An Introduction to Positive Economics*, Weidenfeld & Nicholson, London, 2nd ed.

MARRIOTT, O., 1969, *The Property Boom*, Pan, London.

MEACHER, M., 1971, "Scrooge areas", *New Society*, no. 479.

MEYERSON, M., and BANFIELD, E. C., 1955, *Politics, Planning, and the Public Interest*, The Free Press, New York.

MILL, J. S., 1900, *Principles of Political Economy*, Longmans Green & Co., London, 6th ed.

MUCHNICK, D. M., 1970, *Urban Renewal in Liverpool*, G. Bell & Sons, London.

NORMAN, P., 1971, "Corporation town", *Official Architecture and Planning*, vol. 34, no. 5.

PAHL, R. E., 1975, *Whose city? and Further Essays on Urban Society*, Penguin, Harmondsworth.

POPPER, K. R., 1961, *The Poverty of Historicism*, Routledge & Kegan Paul, London, 3rd ed.

RAPOPORT, A., 1974, *Conflict in the Man-Made Environment*, Penguin, Harmondsworth.

SCHELLING, T. C., 1971, "On the ecology of micromotives", *The Public Interest*, Fall issue.

FURTHER READING FOR CHAPTER 11

A Local Government System, 1973, Open University Press, Bletchley (T241, 7–8).

DAVIES, J. G., 1972, *The Evangelistic Bureaucrat*, Tavistock, London.

DEARLOVE, J., 1973, *The Politics of Policy in Local Government*, CUP.

GOODALL, B., 1972, *The Economics of Urban Areas*, Pergamon, Oxford, chapter 12.

HALL, P., 1974, *Urban and Regional Planning*, Penguin, Harmondsworth, chapter 10.

HARVEY, D., 1973. *Social Justice and the City*, Arnold, London.

LAMBERT, C. and WEIR, D. (eds.), 1975, *Cities in Modern Britain*, Fontana, Glasgow, chapters 6, 7, 8, 9.

NETZER, B., 1974, *Economics and Urban Problems*, Basic Books, New York, 2nd ed.

PAHL, R. E., 1975, *Whose City? and Further Essays on Urban Society*, Penguin, Harmondsworth.

STEWART, M. (ed.), 1972, *The City: Problems of Planning*, Penguin, Harmondsworth.

The System of Control, 1973, Open University Press, Bletchley (DT 201, 19–21).

CHAPTER 12

How Cities Work: an Economic
Viewpoint

MANY of the connections between urban components which we have
already described are the subject of economics. For example, our
Chapters 5 and 9 gave a loose description of the interactions between
people and housing: there are precise economic theories of the
demand for and supply of housing in a local housing market. As
another example, by combining parts of Chapters 5, 6 and 7 we
can deduce that industry in a town will demand workers, some of
whom will want to live in the town, and that where those workers
live will affect the trade of the town's shops: in economic terms,
there is a flow of money out of industry into households as wages,
and out of households into shops as consumers' expenditure.

In addition, there are many important relationships within a town
and between towns which have not so far been mentioned and which
are the subject of economics. Urban policies can create, intentionally
or not, a demand for more labour. Better roads may enable a local
firm to export its goods more easily to other towns, as a result of
which the firm wants to expand its factory. A new industry may
pay higher wages, resulting in the workers changing their consumption patterns and spending more of their incomes on non-local goods
and services, thus reducing the local demand for locally-produced
commodities. And so on.

Knowledge of such relationships is useful if we are to understand
how cities work, essential if we are to make cities work better. The
advantages of formulating them in economic terms are two: there

is a well-established body of economic theory developed for nations which might be applicable to towns and cities, and much of that theory is quantitative. The extra value of quantitative over qualitative theory cannot be overstressed. For example, better communications between a town and the outside world allow both easier importing and easier exporting: whether the net effect will be a gain or loss to the town can be predicted only with quantitative theory.

Those advantages of using economics to study cities, can they be realised? They can, only if we have theories of such relationships which are both true (or, at least, partially true) and which can be quantified. Is our theory thus adequate? It can be argued that it is not, in particular because of the very grave difficulties in applying theories developed for the national economy to the much more open economy of a town.

In this chapter we shall argue that the state of urban economics is stronger than that, and that of the many relevant theories some show great promise of being both true and usable. However, the theories that are thus useful for telling us how cities work are not general theories of the urban economic system but partial theories, each one about the relationships between a few variables. (So we return to the main methodological argument of this book—that in order to learn how cities work we should concentrate on partial systems and not try to construct one general system.)

THE ECONOMIC THEORY IN TWO PARTS

We meet two big difficulties when trying to apply economics to cities. One is that we often have to try to apply standard economic theory to situations for which it was not developed: for example, we want to explain variables such as social structure, rates of building, the demand to live in particular areas, poverty, land use. The other big difficulty is with the treatment of location: causes in the city have effects outside the city, and vice versa. Those two difficulties can be eased by dividing the necessary theory into two parts.

The first part may be called *theories of the urban economy*. These theories include the relationships between economic variables and here we can use the body of well-established economic theory. In this part also we treat the locational issues (in ways which are described later).

The second part may be called *economic theories of urban issues.* Here we put the "non-economic" variables that we might be trying to explain by economic theory. Economic theories of urban issues are the theoretical links between the economic and non-economic variables. Locational issues are kept out of this set of theories.

Let us see how that division of theory would be made. In Chapter 1 we recommended using an *ad hoc* partial system based upon a given problem. Suppose the problem is: the incomes of manual workers in the town are unacceptably low. To start we need to know the causes of low incomes, and the cause-and-effect chains may be set down as a partial system thus:

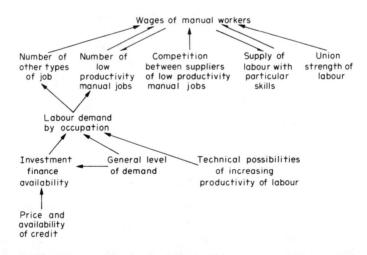

The system (which is much simplified) can be completely described by economic theory: if it included the question of location it would be an example of a theory of the urban economy.

Now consider a different problem, such as: local rivers are unacceptably polluted by industrial and household effluent. The cause-and-effect chains may be described as a partial system as follows.

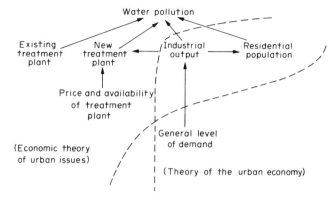

The system (again it is simplified) can be divided into two overlapping systems, as shown. One can be described by economic theory (and includes the locational issues), the other includes both economic and non-economic variables and so must use theories other than standard economics.

LOCATIONAL ISSUES

A city cannot be studied by drawing a boundary around it and ignoring everything outside that boundary: that much we have learnt already in Chapters 3 and 4 about interactions between a city and its region. Now that we are being more precise by applying economic theory to our study of cities, the lesson is even more important: firms in the city buy and sell outside, households in the city may receive much of their income as transfer payments from central government, and lose much of their income in the same way. Such locational issues cannot be ignored. We have said that they will be incorporated in theories of the urban economy, and attempts to do that will be described soon. Before doing that, however, it would help to describe briefly the locational issues in economic terms.

First, how open is the urban economy? The locational difficulties are more important the more open is the economy, so before plunging into the theoretical difficulties we need to know if the openness is significantly great. Casual observation suggests that it is. People (i.e. labour as a factor of production) live in one area, work in another. People (i.e. consumers) earn money in one area and spend it in another. Firms buy inputs from the whole country and often sell their outputs as widely. Central government taxes incomes in London and gives the money as subsidies in Scotland. Systematic observation confirms that. Morrison is one of the few people to have produced a set of social accounts for a town: his data for Peterborough (Morrison, 1973) show that in 1968, total output was about £400 million, imports were £103 million, exports £160 million. So we can take it, without more study, that urban areas *are* very open economies. Hence we need to take the locational issues seriously.

There are four ways in which the urban economy is open, and our theory must take account of all of them. One is the physical ease of factor movements across the urban boundary. Another is the physical ease of personal movements causing changes in the city's net external factor payments. Another is the physical ease with which imports and exports can be traded and be changed. The last is the absence of institutional constraints on some of the economic flows across the urban boundary.

About the first type of openness, Brown (1972) says that many of the problems or urban and regional policy arise "largely because resources of many kinds are neither perfectly mobile nor perfectly immobile between regions, but have a finite degree of mobility which, while it cannot be ignored, is not large in relation to the rate at which patterns of demand and technology change.... In seeking to operate on the location of population and industry, policy is dealing not with quicksilver, but with treacle" (p. 3).

The second type of openness is related to the first. Suppose a person lived and worked in Birmingham, then moved to live and work in London. That is in the first category, a factor movement of treacle speed. Suppose, however, that the person living and working in Birmingham moves house to Worcester but keeps his job in Birmingham. Birmingham has not lost a factor of production, but payments by Birmingham industry for the factor now go outside the city. Suppose that the person gets a job in Worcester but keeps his house in Birmingham. Now Birmingham has lost a factor of production, but it gains factor payments from outside the city. In one case there is a factor movement, in both cases Birmingham's net external factor payments change. Those can be quicksilver changes and the flows of money involved are likely to be significant (e.g. Birmingham C.B., with a 1966 population of 1,066,500 had gained 46,400 of those people by immigration from the rest of Britain in the previous five years, and in that same period had lost 132,500 people by emigration to other parts of Britain, a net loss of 86,100 people to the rest of Britain: Sample Census 1966).

The third cause of openness also involves movements at the quicksilver rate. I was going to buy a television from the local store, but the desired make is not available so I pick up the phone and place an order with the store in the next town. So quickly and easily can I cause an increase in my town's imports. The same might apply to a firm buying inputs. The firm uses a local practice of accountants until that practice proves unable to handle a difficult situation. So the firm transfers its business to a London practice: the local firm starts to import accountancy services.

The fourth cause of openness also involves quicksilver movements, but causes us especial difficulties: moreover, it is not widely recognised, so the difficulties have been little resolved. The cause of the openness may be expressed as follows: a sub-national area is not treated as a self-contained unit for accounting purposes, so its imports and exports need not balance. In that way, a sub-national area is different from a nation and the theory of international economics applicable to the latter cannot be applied to the former. We can see why that is so with an example:

Suppose there are two areas, A and B, and a man in B buys a good from A.

A		B
good produced	£x	man with income
entirely by A	⟵———⟶	entirely from
factors	good	production in B

International trade

Suppose A and B are independent nations. Suppose they use the same currency (£) and maintain a constant exchange rate (that avoids problems of changing relative values). After the purchase, A has a claim on B for £x, which it can use to buy £x of consumer commodities from B, or to buy £x of capital stock in B, or which it can hold as a liquid asset realisable at some date against B.

Inter-urban trade

Suppose A and B are towns. After the purchase, households in A have £x more disposable income, households in B £x less.

1. 'A' households can use the £x to buy £x of commodities produced in B, for which there is not the consumer demand in B (because household income in B has lost £x). If that happens inter-urban trade is analogous to international trade. That is the assumption of many theories of the urban economy. But there is another set of possibilities.

2. Either, the government may levy an extra tax on A of £x and give an extra subsidy to B of £x,

or, parents in A may make a gift of £x to children in B,

or, a firm with plants in A and B and a set of accounts which does not distinguish between the separate plants may reduce payments to A factors by £x and increase payments to B factors by £x, although the outputs of the A and B plants are unchanged. (An international example would be of a multi-national firm switching profits between its national branches in order to minimise its tax payments.) If any of those happens, then A's claim on B is wiped out, as are the excess of income over output in A and the deficiency of income over output in B. If so, inter-urban trade is not analogous with international trade.

So the main difference between international and inter-urban trade involves *transfer payments* (as distinct from payments for resources or for commodities). The important difference is not that such transfers *exist*: there are international transfer payments also. Nor is the important difference that the transfers are *unrecorded*: true, they are recorded in international trade, but that difference is the effect of the crucial difference described below. Nor is it that the transfers are *inexplicable* as the systematic effects of causes: international transfers—e.g. repatriation of immigrants' incomes, Britain's contributions to EEC funds—are not explicable as the effects of economic causes. The important difference is that such transfers are *unconstrained*: there is no need for inward and outward transfers to be equal in the short or the long run, or for a net imbalance of transfer payments to be equalised by an opposite net imbalance of payments for goods, services, or investment. (That has very important consequences for the urban economy which can be summarised as: a town does *not* have to export in order to import. Export or die! might apply to the United Kingdom, but it does not apply to Manchester, or to Scotland.)

The locational issues in trying to apply economics to the study of how cities work can be attributed, we have thus seen, to the openness of the urban economy. But it is useful to keep both formulations—location and openness—of the one phenomenon because the one phenomenon causes us two practical difficulties, one associated with location and one with openness. The difficulty associated with *location* is that economic cause and economic effect might have different locations. The difficulty associated with *openness* is a difficulty in making *quantitative* predictions. A cause in location A will have effects in location A but because of the leaks out of area A the effect will be reduced: because of the leaks into area B, there will be some effect in B.

THEORIES OF THE URBAN ECONOMY

The theory necessary if we are to apply economics to the study of cities we have divided into two parts, and the very difficult locational issues we are going to include in one of the parts—theories of the urban economy. How can that be done? Moreover, if it is done are the resulting theories true and usable? To those questions we now turn.

We can distinguish three different ways of including location in theories of the urban economy: they may be called the economic location approach, the city state approach, and the partial equilibrium approach.

Textbooks on urban economics usually divide approaches to the subject into two—micro-economic and macro-economic. The micro-economic approach focuses on the behaviour of firms and households, on transactions between them, and on how the transactions are modified by government intervention. That approach treats locational issues by an "... attempt to modify neo-classical economics by introducing spatial considerations together with externalities into production and consumption decisions of firms and households" (Hirsch, 1973, p. xvi). The macro-economic approach focuses on aggregate variables (e.g. consumption, investment, exports) and on groups of decision makers (e.g. households, industrial sectors, central and local government). It treats locational issues not in terms of location but in terms of leakages. Hirsch (op. cit. p. 174) distinguishes between the two approaches and their treatments of locational issues as follows. "Whereas in micro-economics, spatial characteristics were viewed in the context of distance and proximity among markets and actors, in macro-economics the important spatial concern is with the openness of the urban economy."

That gives us two approaches to urban economic analysis. From where do we get a third? We divide urban macro-economics into two approaches. One says that although the urban economy is very open, nevertheless there are structural constraints on its external relations so that inflows and outflows are related (e.g. that the urban balance of payments has to be zero); the other approach copes with the openness of the urban economy by assuming that the city's external economic relationships are stable over time. Thus we get three ways of studying the urban economy: the economic location approach (micro-economics), the city state approach (macro-economics, constrained external relations), and the partial equilibrium approach (macro-economics, stable external relationships).

The *economic location approach* treats the urban economy as a *spatial* part of the national economy, the links between the city and the nation being economic flows across space. It tries to give causal explanations of the flows by using theories of location. Location theories try to explain how people choose and change locations (locations to work, live and play and locations from which to buy and to which to sell) by introducing distance into economic theory. To cross space costs time or money, so distance can be included in economic theory as a cost. In that way, neo-classical micro-economics is modified for application to towns and cities.

The *city state approach* treats the city as though it were a nation trading with the rest of the world. Like a nation, the money values of the city's transactions with the rest of the world have to balance, in the long run if not in the short run. The ideal for the urban economist taking the approach is the unified macro-economic theory of a nation, such as that based on Keynes and developed by Stone into a computable model of the British economy (and used for national economic planning in 1965—DEA, 1965). The balance equation equalising imports and exports is one of the cornerstones of such a general theory. It is the necessary equality of inflows and outflows which helps the theorist to build a fairly comprehensive theory of the urban economy: see, for example, Artle's general model of the island economy of Oahu, Hawaii (1965).

The third approach we call the *partial equilibrium approach*: it can be explained as follows. We know that a city is a very open economy, with many unconstrained economic flows across its boundaries. However, now assume that the economic relationships between the city and the rest of the world are held constant: the assumption is not that the flows themselves are constant but that certain hypothesised relationships which explain the flows are constant (e.g. the propensity to import consumer goods out of disposable income). That assumption introduces certain constraints on the openness of the urban economy, constraints which allow us to apply to it macro-economic theory.

We must realise, however, that it is very difficult to apply *general* macro-theories in that way. The reason is the lack of relationship between inflows and outflows. For example, the theory might be that imports of goods and services are a function of area income, but exports do not have to be such as to pay for those imports: exports might be the residual after other components of final demand have claimed the area output, or a function of the GNP of the country of which the city is a part, or some proportion (assumed constant) of area output. That is a weak foundation on which to build comprehensive theories.

However, some of the *partial* theories of the national economy can be applied to cities, for *predicting changes* in some of the city's economic variables. The application is as follows. In order to predict the changes effected by a known cause, we need theories of the relationships between the known cause and its effects. If everything else remains constant (e.g. the city's external economic relationships) we can use partial theories of the national economy to predict the nature of the effects of the cause. The size of the effects depends on the city's external economic relationships (e.g. the leakages): as those remain constant, they can be estimated by surveys, and the results applied to the partial theories. An example will show how changes can be predicted in that way.

Suppose the problem is local unemployment, and the remedy suggested is to bring forward the construction of a new sewage scheme, financed by a loan from central government. Theory suggests the following link between public works schemes and reduced unemployment. Public works employ some men directly (how many are local men depends on the labour available in the local economy) and use resources of cement, equipment, etc. (how much is produced locally depends on the local industries and their capacities). The extra local men who are employed directly and who are employed indirectly (i.e. producing the raw materials, etc.) spend their incomes thus earned (that part of which is not taxed and which they do not save). Some of that expenditure goes on local goods and services (depending on the local propensity to import), which supports more employment (depending on the output per man locally). So we need to estimate, by local surveys and by analysing local data, the local values of spare capacities, marginal propensity to save, etc. Those values depend on the economic relationships between the city and the rest of the world, and if the relationships change then so will the values. But if the remedy of public works is being considered at a time when the economic relationships are the same as when the local values were estimated, then the national economic theory may be applied to the urban economy, using the variables with the local values as estimated, in order to predict the consequences for unemployment. (That is an example which uses the theory of the local multiplier. For a good discussion of that theory and an example of its application, see Brownrigg, 1974.)

We call that approach the partial equilibrium approach because it recognises that the urban economy is part of the rest of the economy, but it keeps the relationships between the part and the whole constant. Changes in the part do not affect significantly the whole, and there is no feedback from changes in the part, through the whole, back to the part. Also, during the period of the analysis, it is assumed that the whole does not change endogenously in such a way as to affect the part (see Lipsey, 1966, p. 499).

So locational issues can be included in theories of the urban economy, in three different ways. We can now move to the second question: are the resulting theories true and usable? Those are stringent tests to which firm answers cannot yet be given. So we shall have to be content with indications of what the answers might be.

The *economic location* approach can be considered in two parts—location theory, and the combination of location theory with micro-economics. Much effort has been spent on location theory but the results so far are not encouraging: either the theory is not yet in a form where it can be tested empirically, or empirical testing has cast doubt on it or been inconclusive. Exception might be made for those location theories embodied in traffic models and shopping models (see, for example Chapters 7 and 10), but even those are of limited applicability, not being transferable from one city to another (Harris, 1968). And there is certainly no general theory of location on the horizon (Richardson, 1969, p. 101). About the combination of location theory and micro-economic theory, Hirsch (1973, p. xvi) says it is "...an exceedingly difficult undertaking in the present state of our knowledge."

The *city state* approach must be rejected because it is based on an assumption—that a city's external payments are constrained in some way—which earlier in this chapter we have shown to be incorrect.

The *partial equilibrium* approach has the strength that it uses partial macro-economic theories which have been tested over many years in the national arena, so that we have good ideas of the conditions in which they hold and in which they do not. However, the approach has two big weaknesses. One is the central assumption that structural economic relationships between the city and the rest of the world are stable. That assumption has been little investigated, but some studies (e.g. Tiebout, 1962; Moses, 1955; Brown, 1972) suggest conditions under which it will be true. The other weakness is that the macro-approach cannot predict locational effects: leakages out of an open economy it can predict, but not where the leakages will make their effects. When such a prediction is wanted, the best hope at present is a combination of the partial equilibrium approach and location theory: a well-known example is the Garin-Lowry model and its variants (see, for example, Wilson, 1974, chap. 11) which combines economic base theory (partial equilibrium) and a gravity model (location theory).

We agreed earlier that it would be useful if we could apply economics to the study of cities, and then we had to take account of the objections that it was not yet possible or valid to apply economic theory to the very open economy of a city. Our account so far has been about economic theories of the urban economy and has shown that the objection is not so strong as to rule out the application, but that it is strong enough to make us act cautiously: in particular, the partial equilibrium approach appears most promising, but it should not be applied in any of the following conditions—an under-developed economy, full employment of productive capacity, big changes in the urban economy, big changes in the rest of the world, changes over a long period.

ECONOMIC THEORIES OF URBAN ISSUES

It remains for us to take account of economic theories of urban issues. It is difficult however to be systematic about these because they are usually *ad hoc*: someone wanted to predict (for example) the demand for housing, so he developed a theory which explained it in terms of employed population and wage income. Because there are many such *ad hoc* theories, all we shall do here is to list some examples:

The demand for shopping floorspace

This is a very simple town planner's theory, that people spend a certain proportion of their incomes in shops, and that to transact a certain amount of retail expenditure a certain area of floorspace is needed. See, for example, the Shankland, Cox report on Ipswich (Shankland, Cox & Associates, 1966).

The demand for housing

This is an even simpler town planner's theory, starting from total population, dividing by average household size, and allowing for vacant dwellings and multi-occupation. See, for example, the Birmingham Structure Plan (1973).

Water use, discharge and pollution

These are explained in terms of the demand by people and by industry—see, for example, Hamilton *et al.* (1966).

Environmental quality

Here, pollution is related to levels of production—see, for example, Isard and Langford (1971).

School district revenue and school district costs

The effect on both of these of changes in final demand sales is predicted by Hirsch by adding two models to the output side of an urban input–output model (Hirsch, 1973).

Urban land requirements

This is another example from Hirsch (1963). He relates changes in land use to changes in final demand, using constant coefficients of acres per dollar of output.

CAN ECONOMICS HELP?

We want to understand how cities work, and perhaps we want to make them work better. The second of those tasks cannot be done properly without the first, and the first task alone is vast. The preceding Chapters 3–11 have been no more than a simple introduction to how cities work: the theories sketched out in those chapters need to be made usable, and then need to be tested to see if they are true. For them to be made usable, the theories need to be made more precise and quantitative. In this last chapter we have asked: Can economics help us to do that? Our short investigation enables us to give a conditional: Yes!

The conditions are that the useful application of economics to urban questions is not well developed, and that the best developments are likely to be in the direction of partial theories. As McKean (1973) puts it, "the practitioners, especially the mathematically inclined, have turned to the hardest or least manageable tasks first, and...the highest priority task now is hypothesis-testing". In more homely terms, we should learn to walk before we try to run.

INDEX TO REFERENCES IN CHAPTER 12

ARTLE, R., 1965, "Planning and growth—a simple model of an island economy: Honolulu, Hawaii", *Regional Science Association Papers*, vol. 15.

Birmingham Structure Plan, 1973, "Draft written statement", Birmingham.

BROWN, A. J., 1972, *The Framework of Regional Economics*, CUP, London.

BROWNRIGG, M., 1974, *A Study of Economic Impact*, Scottish Academic Press, Edinburgh.

Department of Economic Affairs, 1965, *The National Plan*, HMSO, London.

HAMILTON, H. R. *et al.*, 1966, *A Dynamic Model of the Economy of the Susquehanna River Basin*, Batelle Memorial Institute, Columbus, Ohio.

HARRIS, B., 1968, "Quantitative models of urban development", in Perloff, H. S. and Wingo, J. (eds.), *Issues in Urban Economics*, Johns Hopkins, Baltimore.

HIRSCH, W. Z., 1963, "Application of input–output techniques to urban areas", in Barna, T. (ed.), *Structural Interdependence and Economic Development*, Macmillan, London.

HIRSCH, W. Z., 1973, *Urban Economic Analysis*, McGraw Hill, New York.

ISARD, W. and LANGFORD, T. W., 1971, *Regional Input–output Study: Recollections, Reflections, etc.*, Cambridge, Mass.

LIPSEY, R. G., 1966, *An Introduction to Positive Economics*, Weidenfeld & Nicholson, London, 2nd ed.

McKEAN, R., 1973, "An outsider looks at urban economics", *Urban Studies*, vol. 10.

MORRISON, W. I., 1973, "The development of an urban inter-industry model", *Environment and Planning*, vol. 5.

MOSES, L. N., 1955, "The stability of inter-regional trading patterns and input–output analysis", *American Economic Review*, vol. 45.

RICHARDSON, H. W., 1969, *Regional Economics*, Weidenfeld & Nicholson, London.

Sample Census 1966, 1968, Migration regional report—West Midlands Region, HMSO, London.

Shankland, Cox & Associates, 1966, *Expansion of Ipswich*, HMSO, London.

TIEBOUT, C. M., 1962, *The Community Economic Base Study*, supplementary paper no. 16 published by the Committee for Economic Development, New York.

WILSON, A. G., 1974, *Urban and Regional Models in Geography and Planning*, John Wiley, London.

Index

URBAN AND REGIONAL PLANNING SERIES
OTHER TITLES IN THE SERIES